MW00667910

The Road to
MEGA
Success

To Herbert,
wishing you
Mega success
In all you do-

Joan

The Road to MEGA Success

Simple Strategies for Enriching the Bottom Line

Financial Management Guide for Any Business and Industry

Louis G. Hutt, Jr.

Esq., C.P.A.

JOY Publishers

www.louhutt.com

Disclaimer Statement

This publication contains the opinions and ideas of its author. It is intended to provide helpful and informative material on the subject matter covered. It is sold with the understanding that the author and publisher are not engaged in rendering professional services in the book. If the reader requires personal assistance or advice, a competent professional should be consulted.

The author and publisher specifically disclaim any responsibility for any liability, loss or risk, personal or otherwise, which is incurred as a consequence, directly or indirectly, of the use and application of any of the contents of this book.

Copyright © 2008 by Louis Hutt, Jr.

All rights reserved. No part of this publication may be used either in print or electronic form without the written consent of Joy Publishing. Published in the United States by Joy Publishing.

For information regarding personal appearances, interviews or purchases please contact the publisher at:

Joy Publishers, an affiliate of MegaSuccess Partners, Inc.
10500 Little Patuxent Pkwy
Parkview Building, Suite 640
Columbia, Maryland 21044
www.louhutt.com

Editorial and Development: Jadi Keambiroiro
Cover Photo by www.kimberlyportraits.com

Printed in the United States of America at BCP Digital Printing, Inc. • Baltimore, Maryland

ISBN-13   978-0-9817305-0-9

ISBN-10   0-9817305-0-7

First Edition

To my phenomenal wife, Nellie and
my children Mahoganey, Louis and Eboney
who make me proud to be called Dad.

CONTENTS

ACKNOWLEDGEMENTS

Virtually every important breakthrough toward my adolescence, academic and career advancement has been directly or indirectly attributable, to my wife Nellie, and my parents Joyce and Louis G. Hutt, Sr. They paved the way for me to reach the next level.

My wife's unwavering love, support and companionship has been a source of strength through life's highs and lows. She has been in my corner privately and publicly to encourage, console and advise. Nellie's belief in me and her many personal sacrifices enabled me to pursue my dreams. Even with a demanding professional career of her own as an Appeals Judge she also has been a wonderful and loving mother to our children. Looking back over a lifetime, my wife has certainly been the best thing that ever happened for me.

Despite very humble beginnings, I was also blessed with a mother and father who loved, nurtured and educated me. They would not rest until they had indeed prepared me for life's journey. My mother taught me how to reason and think for myself rather than just go along just to get along with the crowd. She prodded me to assess life's situations and make personal decisions based on simple principles and sound values. She also grilled me on the golden rule to treat other people the way I would want to be treated. On the other hand, my father focused on life long lessons involving personal integrity, responsibility and dependability. Rather than rely solely on words, he demonstrated these ideals by setting a positive example everyday as a husband, father and doer.

I know without the time, attention and love of my wife, mother and father I would not be where I am today. Very deservedly, I dedicate this book in their honor.

Of all the personal ambitions I have sought to fulfill, composing a book certainly ranks very high on the list. My supportive wife Nellie gave me the green light to embark on this project while we were on a long overdue vacation in the Virgin Islands. However, I seriously doubt at the time she had any idea finishing this work would become my obsession. Her accommodation, patience and support throughout was remarkable.

I was also very fortunate to have a core team of advisors who not only participated in the vetting of ideas and content, but continually reassured me that the end was in sight. My daughter Mahoganey Hutt Butler and associate Mary Kay Boler guided my efforts from the beginning to the end of the process. On the other hand, my son Louis G. Hutt, III, only a relatively recent graduate of the Olin School of Business at Washington University, challenged my conceptual thinking. He forced me to seek to find the simplest common denominator to explain financial and business approaches. My youngest daughter Eboney soon to graduate from high school was indispensable as well. She was my biggest fan and cheerleader.

I would not have been in a position to expound on the fundamentals of business and financial management had my college accounting professor, Robert Virgil, PhD not chosen to mentor and befriend me. More than simply a teacher, he served as a personal coach. Confirmation from someone at the upper echelon of my field of interest to the effect that I could indeed succeed in the profession, was the spark that sent me on a tear. I went on to broaden my professional horizon from not just business but to law as well, and passed both the CPA and Bar exams.

To my principal business partners, I also owe much thanks. They helped make possible a rewarding private practice with countless opportunities to work hand and hand with a wide range of entrepreneurs, high level business executives, and tax exempt organizations. W. Charles Bennett became one of my closet friends in college. Most of all, we came to respect each other's academic commitment and work ethic. We graduated and started careers together at Ernst and Young. Later, we decided to join together to fill a perceived void in the market for management consulting and technical accounting advice. The confidence he had to step out with me on faith and start a business still amazes me.

I have also been blessed to have my younger brother, Kevin T. Hutt, Sr. as a business partner. Kevin was our firm's first full-time employee out of college. The star recruit proved worthy in every way imaginable. He not only leveraged the training and work experience professionally, but has become a highly-respected leader and volunteer in the community at large. I am proud to recognize my brother for helping making this project a reality.

There were many others both in and outside of my firm who too made valuable contributions to this endeavor. My senior associate, Keith Price, assumed a portion of my day-to-day office responsibilities in order to afford me spare time on the job to finish writing. I also would be remiss not to recognize Stanley Tucker and other partners of MMG Ventures for first commissioning me to facilitate an entrepreneurial training for many of their portfolio clients.

Additionally, I must extend special thanks to David Allen, Kenneth Cooper, Barry Glassman, Timothy Smoot and Monica Wood for offering helpful advice and counsel. Last but far from least, Paulette Robinson and Jadi Keambiroiro were absolutely magnificent in providing professional guidance and feedback.

INTRODUCTION

Cultivating a profitable business is not always linked to the skills or educational training a business owner or decision-maker receives in school. Many secrets of success lie in the application and exercise of judgment in real time and under pressure. In this view, the most daunting challenge faced by entrepreneurs is of the financial variety. Proficiency in financial management often separates the winners and losers. Having a conceptual understanding of the financial framework for sound business management is essential.

Are you overly dependent on your accountants to understand the meaning of the financial data? Have you ever been shocked by a potential investor's unfavorable conclusion about the financial strengths and weaknesses of your business? Do you feel uncomfortable navigating between different financial statements?

Are you unable to identify critical financial information for your business? Do you struggle to convert profit potential into real financial returns? Is cash flow a chronic and crippling problem? Is your legal infrastructure weak and ill-fitted to your business model?

ROAD TO MEGASUCCESS

If you answer in the affirmative to any of the questions noted earlier, *The Road to MegaSuccess* will be a guiding light. The book is tailored for the entrepreneur who has experienced anxiety, frustration, or trauma in building a financially viable business. It demystifies the conventional financial methods of business management, so that the average person can easily understand. Deliberately designed to be an easy read, this book will help to increase the odds for your business success.

Key concepts, issues and challenges will be addressed from an entrepreneur's perspective. Simply stated, I discuss how to make, measure and maximize money from operating a business venture. The spotlight is on best practices for entrepreneurs financially and on strategies designed to maximize financial returns. For most entrepreneurs operating on a relatively limited capital base this knowledge is crucial. They cannot afford to make an expensive error in judgment and expect to recover. Faced with countless financial perils, business owners have to be vigilant about putting into operation best practices.

Entrepreneurs must be proactive about the handling of financial affairs of their business. The disposition of an armchair spectator could be fatal. Accordingly, the aim of *The Road to MegaSuccess* serves to strengthen entrepreneurs' financial capabilities and sensitize them to potential hazards.

Just as preparation and discipline are germane to the ultimate success of a pro athlete and the team, the same focus can improve an entrepreneur's ability to maximize his or her company's bottom line. Many pro athletes recognized long ago, to get to the top of their respective sports—be it the Super Bowl, the Stanley Cup, the NBA

Finals, or the Masters—personal development and self-improvement must be part of their everyday lives. Most successful entrepreneurs also recognize that their overall success is directly tied to how well their companies are prepared to perform and operate financially.

ENRICHING THE BOTTOM LINE

In the final analysis, the focus of this book will be on improving the bottom line. This mission will be pursued by explaining financial techniques in the most straightforward fashion using plain language. Guidance and direction will be offered on how best to navigate real life financial management decisions, all the while concentrating on principles of proven financial planning and management solutions that will work for large, mid-sized, as well as small companies.

We begin with a reflection on financial difficulties commonly encountered by entrepreneurs in making a profit. Through the use of illustrations and familiar analogies, entrepreneurs will be placed in the shoes of seasoned business veterans and glean how they might formulate useful strategies. The journey will stretch from the stage of business infancy to maturity.

Other intricacies of financial management include tracking the flow of resources—whether invested, borrowed, or earned. If you do not know or track the flow of dollars in and out of your business, your company is destined to under-perform or, worse, to fail. Entrepreneurs, business aspirants, CEOs, and managers should find the coverage of methods for instilling peak performance extremely valuable.

Rest assured, in order to master the fundamentals you need not be a mathematician or Certified Public Accountant. In this book, a dozen chapter titles express the thrust of what I describe as, *Simple Strategies for Enriching the Bottom Line.* These steps reflect the keys to financial strength from the critical perspectives of investors, bankers, and professionals who routinely advise business owners. In addition, and perhaps more importantly, they offer a map for keeping a business in top shape financially.

From a strategic perspective I strive to offer a model that will focus on the financial implications of certain business decisions. The guidelines range from short-hand methods of determining breakeven to ascertaining the financing needs of your business. These skills are crucial for every business owner whose goal is to attract capital and maximize profitability.

PROFITABLE GROWTH MANAGEMENT

At the end of the day, the business objective shared by virtually every company is growth and expansion. With size, there is hope for greater financial muscle and operating stability. Too often, however, entrepreneurs and their key decision-makers miss the real target, namely, profitable growth. This book will help keep you focused on the separate roles of *growth* versus *profit.*

Intuitively most business people think of growth without fully contemplating the financial challenges that accompany it. Growth typically means not only increased sales, but more locations, larger staff, additional equipment and higher financing requirements. Unless a company adequately prepares to meet these demands, growth can be financially counterproductive.

Companies that are truly financially progressive, emphasize profit planning and growth control. Entrepreneurs quickly learn from experience that achieving profit while growing is not an easy proposition. It requires implementing a well-conceived and delicately synchronized business plan. The financial components of the plan are integral to success. The fundamentals will be covered in this book. Fortunately, they apply to most any business regardless of size or industry.

The importance of each key building block will be illuminated through a practical case study that should ring a bell with most readers. The Journey, found at the beginning of each chapter, features two fictional entrepreneurs, BJ Armstrong of Matrix, Inc., and Taylor Made of Potomac, LLC. Whether you are an aspiring or a seasoned entrepreneur, most business people should find it easy to identify with their plight. The text of each chapter then proceeds to offer relevant alternatives and solutions.

ACCELERATING THE JOURNEY

Along the way I will demonstrate that memorizing numbers, balances, or figures, is by no means essential to achieving high financial returns. In fact, I only know of a few highly successful entrepreneurs who expound detailed financial information contained in the body of their company's financial statements. On the other hand, they have a commanding knowledge and grasp of the fundamental financial parameters of their business.

Rarely will a banker or investor be inclined to invest capital in a company unless the CEO has a thorough understanding of the finances of their business. With rare exception, entrepreneurs have to be prepared to run the gamut and when necessary, explain the financial performance and condition of their company. This may range from providing an overview of operating assets and liabilities, and a breakdown of current and past net earnings or loss.

In the final analysis, you need not be a financial expert to be successful in business. However, the odds of success are much greater for those able to interpret basic financial statements and comprehend their meaning. Accordingly, the goal of this book is to help the reader build the necessary skill set.

On first thought, the idea of reading a book about financial management may seem a bit intimidating, if not overwhelming. However, you need not worry, as each of the topics will be reduced to simple common principles like those we live by in making personal financial decisions. I am confident the journey you are about to take will leave you better equipped to accelerate financially along *The Road to MegaSuccess.*

CHAPTER ONE
Prepare for MegaSuccess...
Set the Right Course

| *The Journey* |

AFTER TEN YEARS IN THE WORKFORCE, BJ Armstrong launched his own business. Matrix Corporation distributes housekeeping, cleaning, and maintenance supplies including detergents, waxes, and other industrial cleansers. In addition, Matrix sells restaurant and dining room supplies including glasses, tableware, napkins, and coffeepot filters. Several years ago the company introduced a commercial maintenance and cleaning services division to offer customers a complete solution under one roof.

Like most entrepreneurs BJ struggled to survive during his initial years of business. Producing a positive cash flow and bottom line profit on a consistent basis was difficult. For the first two years expenses outpaced revenues. In the third year, when the company finally generated a profit, cash flow became erratic. Payments to suppliers frequently fell behind and jeopardized the company's credit standing. Had BJ's family not stepped in to assist with a short-term loan, the company would not have survived this very difficult period.

Seven years later, BJ's company is considered one of the top ten restaurant and cleaning supply distributors in the Atlantic coast region and employs twenty-five people. Its customer base includes an assortment of mid-to-large-size chain restaurants, hotels, and motels. Having reached a milestone in the development of his business BJ is grappling with how to take his company to the next level in a highly competitive market.

Having a command of the fundamentals of financial management is a tremendous advantage in growing a profitable business. Even the most creative business strategy is bound to languish without strong leadership from a financial perspective. Setting the right course is at least half the battle in achieving Mega Success.

SELF-STARTERS

Are you a self-taught business novice or veteran? You have managed to build a very successful business but secretly continue to struggle with the financial aspects of business management. Could it be that, although you are happy to receive them routinely, your accountant's financial statements have little value, and you have struggled to connect the data in a meaningful way?

CORPORATE PROS

Are you currently a business decision-maker within a company who has been saddled with significant financial management responsibility? Under your watch, profits have been sporadic despite exceptional growth in sales revenues. Perhaps your company's growth has stalled due to lack of access to capital. Has deciphering the financial jargon used by bankers and investors made it difficult to confidently negotiate financing?

ENTREPRENEUR CONVERTS

In your prior career, were you the expert in your field with a well established business or organization, but now find you are a novice in managing your own business? Do you feel comfortable with the dynamics of buying, selling, and marketing your business, but feel inadequate when it comes to interpreting financial statements, projecting cash flow, and managing profits?

If you identify with any of the profiles listed rest assured you are not alone. Many high-flying achievers in business have traveled the same road. For them the key to overcoming such challenges was the exposure and utilization of proven solutions for managing the bottom line. Truth is, if you never learn the art of the trade you will always be climbing the mountain.

Even with a MBA, business experience, and professional guidance navigating the financial affairs of a business can be treacherous. The myriad of conditional "what if" decisions can be overwhelming. Textbook knowledge alone will only carry you so far. To make it over the hump, you must have certain critical insights help to exercise sound judgment.

Most seasoned decision-makers agree financial planning and business management are their greatest challenge. Stress, confusion, and frustration stem from struggles to stimulate growth and profit simultaneously. All agree a simple roadmap to outline the entrepreneurial journey could make a major difference in achieving success.

The Road to MegaSuccess is the answer to the business decision-maker's quandary. Irrespective of whether you are inexperienced or seasoned, the practical lessons, concepts and real life experiences presented in *The Road to MegaSuccess* will help accelerate your ascent through the ranks of the business world. In substance this book offers a simple model for navigating the hurdles along the way to growing a profitable business whether the overall economy happens to be strong or weak.

My objective is to make entrepreneurs and decision-makers at all levels, more confident, knowledgeable, and capable of profitably managing the bottom line. By the end of this book you will be better equipped with practical knowledge and skill proficiency in financial management. Let us start with a conceptual overview of what to expect.

CHAPTER HIGHLIGHTS:

+ Straight Talk

+ Financial Strategy

+ Planning for Profit

+ Overcoming Roadblocks

+ Key Milestones

+ Competitive Will Power

A STRAIGHT PATHWAY

Here's the proverbial "real deal"... healthy profits require two main ingredients, a well-defined financial strategy and a strong support system. This fundamental premise naturally assumes the venture under consideration offers products or services that are both in demand and command value in the marketplace.

For most entrepreneurs and CEOs of growing businesses bringing a product to market is the least of their worries. Their strength and talent usually lies in sales and marketing. On the other hand, the thing that keeps them up at night is financial direction. Deciding on a route that will most likely lead to stability and profitability is every decision makers quandary. This book is primarily intended to be a ray of hope to this audience.

> *Managing profit requires a well-defined financial strategy and a strong support system.*

Notwithstanding their ability to formulate novel marketing ideas, gauge industry innovation and work effectively with people, secretly many people who are in charge are extremely apprehensive about managing the financial side of the house. The good news…business leaders with only limited background in finance and accounting can become highly effective in financial management with two things on their side, a thorough understanding of financial fundamentals and a simple roadmap.

Those I hope to reach will be fascinated to discover how basic and straight forward the logic behind supposedly complex areas of financial and business management. When these concepts are conveyed in familiar context, I believe most business people are capable of grasping them and elevating their confidence. At the end of the day, I want to put you in position, figuratively speaking, to win a gold medal for financial leadership. In business, a working knowledge of financial concepts and techniques is a great advantage.

At the core much of what is commonly referred to as a financial strategy is simply another way to describe what will be the normal progression of business development. In the early stages growing businesses are forced to take major risks and justifiably must be primarily concerned about preserving capital. To improve the odds it is best to have a straight forward plan that pinpoints financial goals and benchmarks. In other words, you need a sound financial model to steer your decisions.

To achieve profitability, financial management capabilities have to be developed quickly in order to avoid careless, costly, and sometimes crippling mistakes. Even in the normal course of events, the financial resources of growing businesses will be stretched to the limit. During these periods, survival may hinge on how well resources are invested, managed and monitored.

For a CEO of any size company to successfully drive profits the business must devise a solid financial strategy.

In the business realm financial planning and preparation covers a lot of ground ranging from determining breakeven sales revenues, business financing to pricing strategies. With this in mind, my main focus will be on equipping you to be proactive and less prone to crisis decision making. In essence, I want you to be prepared to solve rather than agonize over critical business and financial situations encountered.

To be response ready, financial decision-makers need a built in capacity to take frequent readings of profit, cash flow and net worth. These measurements enable them as well as outside third parties to evaluate the success or failure of current strategies and tactics. Fairly or unfairly, financial outcomes dictate the perceived strength or weakness of a business in the eyes of the outside world. With this high degree of significance I would be remiss not to offer in this book plenty of tips on how to refine your company's financial profile.

GEMS OF WISDOM

Many people are able to personally identify with the old adage, "If I knew yesterday what I know today, I would be much further ahead financially." In business, this truth is self evident as well. We all know lessons learned could be extremely valuable the second time around. On the other hand, it is not always necessary to come around again or face the brink of financial disaster to acquire this special knowledge.

The Road to MegaSuccess is a business playbook filled with gems of wisdom. For instance, the next chapter focuses on the most common traps that plague growing businesses and how to avoid them. Financial issues classically arise from the very start and if left unresolved will impede many companies from moving to the next level. To highlight the most effective strategies real world examples involving top tier companies will be provided throughout the book.

In many respects what you will be exposed to should be quite comforting. It may be consoling to know you are not alone in the struggle to find ways to profitably manage a business. The dynamics are perplexing and sometimes overwhelming even to the high flying superstars. However by closely examining their plight, you will be able to acquire the secrets to success through their trials and tribulations as well as your own. In all cases, your life savings and personal wealth need not be at risk to gain these precious insights. Only a relatively small number of entrepreneurs have the financial capacity to rebound after making a gross error in judgment.

Fortunately, some of the best practices in business management are found in common sense principles based on life experience. In real life people rarely make a major personal investment without first doing their homework. For instance, at the time of purchasing residential property, most people research the neighborhood, school district, area recreational facilities, and other amenities. The average buyer will go so far as to investigate recent sales of similar homes in the neighborhood. They know instinctively the best ways to size up a fair price before signing on to such a major commitment.

In business, financial decision making need not be much different than purchasing residential property. Prior to outlaying resources to contract new hires, buy equipment or expand facilities the merits of the deal should be carefully evaluated. Essentially you must weight the potential financial benefits and financial benefits against costs. In most business courses this analytical model is conveniently referred to as a cost benefit analysis. I hope to make you very comfortable using this and other fundamental approaches to decide when, where, and how to deploy the resources of your business.

> *Entrepreneurs who fail to make business decisions methodically or in a vacuum raise the risk of their demise.*

Entrepreneurs who fail to make decisions methodically or make them in a vacuum increase the risk of their demise. On the contrary, when they rely on sound reasoning and proven business practices many of the inherent risks in operating a business drop substantially.

CRITICAL MILESTONES

Cultivating a profitable business is analogous to running a long marathon. Just like distance runners should identify in advance possible turning points in a race and contemplate how to keep pace—so too entrepreneurs and other key decision makers should size up the roadway leading to business success.

Much of advance preparation of a runner involves judging time, distance and landscape. Similarly, using rules of thumb in business is akin to evaluating a long distance course. Like marathoners, entrepreneurs have to gauge the journey in order to properly manage their resources and maintain competitive intensity.

Establishing concrete milestones will keep a company on track operationally and financially.

Your game plan should include different markers as reference points. Even when entrepreneurs and managers start with a coherent business plan it may be necessary from time to time to deviate due to exigencies and unforeseen developments. As the journey progresses, the only way to get back on track is to key on specific milestones. The most critical ones are identified operationally or financially.

The junctures that confirm the right pathway to a healthy bottom line and financial stability should be set forth from the start. Strategically, the entrepreneurial marathon is made up of distinct stages, each of which poses a set of very unique challenges.

FIRST LEG

- Form Legal Entity
- Secure Start-Up Funding
- Accelerate Cash Flow and Sales Growth
- Procure adequate Operating Facilities and Equipment
- Implement Transaction Review, Approval and Authorization
- Establish Protocols

SECOND LEG

- Redefine Profit and Tax Planning Objectives
- Upgrade Financial Accounting and Reporting Systems
- Standardize Performance Measures
- Attract Competent Qualified Personnel
- Form Strategic Alliances and Key Business Relationships
- Evaluate Creative Financing Alternatives

THIRD AND FINAL LEG

- Manufacture Profitable Sales Growth
- Build Infrastructure to Support Expansion
- Adopt Risk Management Programs and Practices
- Devise Strategies for Wealth Accumulation
- Implement Exit or Succession Plan

A well-labeled roadmap can be invaluable in times of stress. It not only helps minimize risk of making a wrong turn but assures a quick recovery. Based on a concrete set of milestones, entrepreneurs ought to be free to concentrate on managing business strategies and solutions. Accordingly, each chapter in The Road to MegaSuccess is framed to help you define the most critical milestones along the way to success.

THE POWER CONNECTION

At some point in the journey every viable business requires greater access to capital to support growth. For the most part growth feeds on capital. When your marketing and sales efforts bear fruit through name recognition, customer loyalty and business reputation, a higher demand for your products and services will usually necessitate expanding business infrastructure. In order to meet this need capital from the outside is usually required.

Every viable business needs access to capital.

Growth capital is commonly sought to underwrite increases in expenditures for additional staff, equipment, and facilities. Being better equipped assures the same quality of customer service will be maintained despite a much larger customer base. However, when these preparations are delayed for too long, growth can be a destabilizing force.

While some entrepreneurs spend an exorbitant amount of time and energy frantically attempting to lure capital, savvy executives take a strategic approach to meeting their needs. Simply put, they survey the underwriting criteria of the most eligible financiers and then methodically prep their business to pass the litmus test at just the right time.

To be a strong advocate before prospective financiers you must understand the lingo. The basic financial jargon used by bankers, investors and other stakeholders may otherwise be intimidating if not confusing. In order to function in the world of financing it pays for entrepreneurs and CEOs to be conversant.

While business terms such as net income, profit margin and cash flow differ slightly from common everyday vocabulary, they generally speak to many of the same concerns people must confront everyday. For instance, when making a purchase of a major appliance most people pause to assess the cost of capital. In essence, they inquire about the interest rate and, after all payments, how much they will pay over the original purchase price. In turn, the seller will most assuredly run a credit check, ask for verification of employment and other information to establish credit.

The mechanics of processing a business loan are not materially different than purchasing a major home appliance. Your concerns as a business owner center around whether borrowed funds can be used productively and if so, at what cost. On the other hand, the prospective financier will want as much assurance as possible that your company will have the ability to meet repayment obligations. As you will find later in this book securing financing is the consummate business negotiation.

Attracting capital is both science and art. The science, of course, encompasses technical standards and measures that shed light on the financial capacity of a business to shoulder regular monthly payments. On the other hand, the artistic elements entail strategically building relationships and connections that could open doors down the road. Understanding these tidbits holds many secrets to profitable growth and expansion. Because the financing process is so important and sometimes elusive, it will receive extensive coverage in this book.

NAVIGATING THE NUMBERS

Naively, many business people underestimate their ability to navigate their way through financial data. As accountants we are largely to blame because the format and the labels ascribed to various totals and subtotals listed in financial statements are foreign to most people. The pertinent information sometimes appears so convoluted that people simply give up. On the contrary knowing the key concepts will eliminate needless frustration.

When it comes to understanding a conventional set of financial statements I recommend entrepreneurs and CEOs focus extensively on the big picture. Later, I will breakdown the true meaning and significance of three widely used types of financial statements and explain in laymen's terms the key parts of each that are most important to grasp. You will probably come away wondering how you ever allowed yourself to be so confused.

Perhaps just as important as understanding financial statements in order to be on equal footing with investors and other financiers, I want to help you discover how to get the most from them for purposes of assessing performance and making business decisions. With a constant onslaught of complex questions and emerging developments, an entrepreneur, CEO or manager cannot afford to ignore the practical applications and value of information contained in them.

In addition to conventional financial reporting, I will focus on a handful of financial models that are extremely useful in monitoring profitability and cash flow. Understanding these models holds the possibility of creating a whole new paradigm for managing your business. Their applications will most assuredly help you to establish the appropriate financial targets such as breakeven sales revenues and defining financing requirements. In the end, I want to enable you to make wiser more beneficial financial decisions.

Ultimately, the financial toolbox you will have access to by reading this book should serve to help enrich your business bottom line. However, positioning to get there will mean investing handsomely in upgrading you financial operating methods. You must have the built-in flexibility to shift gears throughout the year while remaining on course to meet defined profit objectives.

Rarely does a business achieve profits on a consistent basis just by happenstance. A precursor to success is a clear financial strategy. With this in mind, every CEO should possess the skills to navigate the numbers. No well meaning business executive would want to authorize purchase of equipment, approve funding for bonuses or sign on to the acquisition of commercial real estate, only to discover the commitment was in truth, unaffordable. Likewise, it would be counter-productive to authorize a sales contract that did not offer a reasonable probability of income equal to or greater than expected outlays.

> *A CEO with no interest in financial affairs may spend recklessly and unknowingly lead their company down a path of failure.*

In order to fully mobilize a business, there is no substitute for your own knowledge and proficiency in financial management. As the ultimate decision maker your command and understanding of financial rewards and risks will decide whether your company will maintain a leading edge. For all intents and purposes, your business' financial well being will be under your tutelage.

Entrepreneurs and CEOs alike discover quickly—especially in fast-growing companies—it is virtually impossible to keep track financially unless you have a thorough understanding of what is really going on.

THE END GAME

In terms of intensity, leadership in business is comparable to coaching competitive sports. The mental and physical preparation required to excel are all consuming. Focus and supervision of the field play is also very demanding. To achieve success in the end, thorough planning, keen judgment and systematic control are essential.

In high level sports and business winning requires a highly choreographed and unified effort. The role of the coach and the CEO is to smooth out the rough edges and, in the end, pull it all together and make it happen. Whether in business or in sports the chief decision maker is ultimately held accountable for the performance of the team. This is an awesome responsibility.

From evaluating competition, selecting personnel, mapping strategy, to play calling, it pays for the chief decision maker to be a scholar of the game. By comparison, leaders in business are essentially their company's designated head coach. The success or failure of the business rests on their shoulders.

Just like in sports, there is a premium on head coaches who have the skill to edge out a tough win despite adversity. Coaches and CEOs share this challenge in common as well as much appreciation for a durable game plan capable of surviving the most rugged tests. Your financial plan and strategy is essentially a game plan.

To produce positive results a financial strategy must be dynamic in nature, that is, able to withstand shock and pressure. Sound planning embraces economic variances due to employee turnover, salary adjustments, financing limitations and competitive regulatory and other significant pressures that may surface. A predetermined resolution

Heading a business is like coaching in sports, you are responsible for readying your team in every aspect of the game.

normally requires monetary investment contingency measures, and back up preparation.

In *The Road to MegaSuccess* I will also speak about holistic financial planning from a best and worst case perspective. Undoubtedly most every industry and business must be poised financially to endure up and down cycles. The key to remaining in the winner's circle is a simple model for enriching the bottom line.

Before illustrating a simple approach for boosting cash flow and profits, the next chapter will discuss the common pitfalls entrepreneurs, CEOs and managers should steer clear of at all times.

Notable Reflections at a Glance

→ Building a financially viable business is not about finding shortcuts.

→ Life lessons offer a wealth of guidance on how to manage a profitable business.

→ Profitable operations require a holistic financial strategy and strong support system.

→ Growth financing follows successful business development

→ Navigating financial statements should be as much a conceptual as a detail exercise.

→ A mark of good business coaching is winning in the face of adversity.

CHAPTER TWO
Evade the Fault Line…
Avoid the Classic Pitfalls

| *The Journey* |

BJ Armstrong reconnects with his former college class-mate, Taylor Made, at their 10-year class reunion. The old friends discover they are both entrepreneurs and find themselves trading experiences of business ownership.

Even in college both BJ and Taylor dreamed of owning their own businesses. Straight out of school Taylor accepted a position with a technology consulting company. Five years ago, she launched her own company, Potomac Technologies.

Potomac provides software development, IT consulting and technical oversight to businesses and government agencies. Its customized software consists primarily of inventory management, distribution, and data processing applications.

After overcoming three years of anemic sales growth, Potomac's annual volume peaked at $5 million and has been flat for the past two years. In addition, the company's profits have declined steadily. Taylor has been struggling to pinpoint the reasons for the change of fortune.

Looking forward, Taylor expects increased competitive pressure from overseas companies offering lower-cost outsourcing. In fact, she is worried about losing two major accounts to overseas competitors. Taylor shares her anxieties and seeks BJ's advice.

Knowing how to make a business succeed requires understanding how to prevent it from falling short financially or failing altogether. Sadly, instances of business failure or underperformance are all too common.

For new businesses the highest risk of failure is within the first four years of operations.[1] Conversely, while not necessarily worried about failure per se, established companies confront the threat of financial decline and loss well into maturity.

Entrepreneurs in newly minted businesses must learn to quickly climb the learning curve. The difficulty in achieving and maintaining profits partly lies in scarcity of time. Most entrepreneurs are stretched thin between fine tuning selling tactics, juggling expenditures, hiring staff and supervising operations. In practice, very little energy is left over for financial and strategic planning once the business is out of the gate.

Managing success in the early stage of business development is further challenged by a limited capital base. While business growth has a hefty appetite for capital sources of funding are practically nonexistent for start-up ventures struggling to achieve profitability. The journey from survival to stability to prosperity poses a unique set of different obstacles and threats with each phase of progress.

For companies that reach puberty and beyond the greatest hurdle is to produce a profit on a consistent basis. In order to do so, they must contend with intensified competition, escalating expenses, emerging regulations, and periodic turnover in work force. While struggling through these conditions boosting cash flow and profits becomes a daunting task. For CEOs and other key decision makers to keep on track financially, they must rely on a healthy set of precepts.

Regardless of seniority, size or industry the secret to enriching the bottom line for any business has multiple layers ranging from financial, operational and strategic, to sales and marketing. In this chapter, I will highlight the most pivotal and serious obstacles that must be overcome from a management perspective to minimize risks of business failure and financial decline.

CHAPTER HIGHLIGHTS:

→ Financial Missteps

→ Mismanaged Growth

→ Non-Profitable Business Model

→ Crisis Mentality

→ Weak Oversight

→ Progressive Complacency

→ Lack of Planning

SHAKE THE MIRAGE

Managing the financial affairs of a business can be very similar to riding a roller coaster—sharp twists and turns at neck-breaking speed.

To endure the daily ride, you must have a systematic approach that both measures and manages the flow of resources. This is not only a key to making money in business but to building wealth through business ownership.

Without a monitoring system to gain an accurate read on the flow of money, most businesses would operate in a grandiose illusion of profit. Dollars could hurry in but not at a rate equal to mounting expenses. As most people realize, cash in the bank is by no means a sign of profitability or viability. A holistic view of revenue and expenses is the best determinate. Otherwise, one can easily be misled.

Entrepreneurs stand to lose potential investors if they fail to adequately document their financial standing. In some cases, lucrative ventures fail to secure necessary capital simply because financial information is not readily available. Sometimes, problems that could be solved through basic price and cost adjustments go unabated in the absence of updated financial reporting. When the financial results of business decisions are unknown a small leak in the financial model can reach crisis proportion in no time.

It is hardly a surprise that highly successful companies rely heavily on a variety of financial support systems to navigate through troubled waters. If you are in business for any length of time you will find different types of tools are necessary to grow profits. If your toolbox lacks the right instruments your business is more susceptible to financial upheaval. In many such instances, simply having access to financial information will be the saving grace. It may allow you to bypass the fault line and steer performance in a positive direction.

Just as a computer operating system needs a reliable server to collect and dispatch data, a business needs a dependable accounting system to track financial activity. Having the ability to assemble and analyze specific financial data in real time is essential for wise decision making. If your server is malfunctioning your operating and decision-making could be seriously skewed. For this same reason, CEOs have to be just as vigilant about the condition, quality and fine tuning of their financial support systems.

Imagine bidding on a major customer contract without accurate cost information. Perhaps you receive the wrong data or the information most crucial to your decision is buried in reams of payroll reports, sales invoices, or supplier billing statements. In these situations, frustrations and confusion can lead to decision-making based solely on gut instinct. If so, a business will be at high risk to make grave financial missteps.

Managing the financial and business activities of a private company can be compared to a roller coaster ride—plenty of sharp twists and turns at break-neck speed.

The reliability of your accounting system will influence virtually every business decision you make. Decision makers at virtually all levels are less likely to make wise choices with unreliable or incomplete financial information. Hard numbers are crucial when determining, for example, whether to increase payroll, purchase new equipment, order inventory, or extend customer credit. These decisions should not be made on a whim. For optimal results a business owner and his or her managers must have access to all the pertinent facts.

Documenting the state of your company's financial health is also critical in attracting capital. Rarely will a bank, investor or creditor extend funding to a business that is unable to supply conventional financial statements. Financiers are persuaded not only by the quality of entrepreneurs' business experience, industry knowledge and profit strategies, but their competence in financial management as well. Lenders and investors know that financial oversight dictates a borrower's future ability to comply with future payment and reporting obligations.

Finally, virtually every company must utilize a regimen of financial checks and balances. With growth and expansion comes a greater need to verify daily cash receipts, purchases, customer collections and other financial transactions through various control mechanisms. It is practically impossible for top brass to personally inspect and confirm these activities. Internal checks and balances serve to raise a red flag which indicates things may have been mishandled. Most controls consist of routine self and cross checks. A wide array of financial controls will be discussed in much greater detail later in the book.

REJECT CRIPPLING GROWTH

In retrospect decade old reports of automobiles that revved up without any pressure on the accelerator were quite frightening. These incidents were described as "unattended acceleration." Although the ensuing investigations failed to confirm the existence of any structural defects, the label aptly captured the image of a vehicle taking off on its own beyond the control of the operator.

The term unattended acceleration, could readily apply to a business experiencing spiraling and uncontrollable sales growth. Unfettered sales growth may have the same effect as an out of control vehicle, namely, placing the business operator in a helpless management predicament and at risk financially.

Many companies, feeling pressure to perform profitably, are often tempted to allow sales growth to rev up to dangerous levels. Contributing to these situations are accepting high-risk unproductive contracts just to bring in new business, or signing on customers with a questionable credit history for the sake of increased market share. In the long term, most of these quick fix solutions prove to be counterproductive and detrimental financially.

Operating capacity has to coincide with growth. Otherwise, infrastructure failures are likely. Trouble signs include sudden jump in the incidence of equipment failures such as computer software crashes. Similarly, the usage and cost of material and labor may begin to skyrocket.

The survival of a business will be in jeopardy whenever sales growth is permitted to sprawl aimlessly.

Extreme growth may be the result of self-destructive pricing policies. New business derived strictly based on price may create an illusion of real growth. While razor thin price margins work for high volume businesses, this approach is not suited for all. Low-ball pricing is prone to financial loss especially where costs of labor and material are subject to wide swings and fluctuations. In essence, using overly aggressive competitive pricing simply to win market share usually poses serious financial risks.

Growth fueled on the backs of chronically late paying customers is also counterproductive. A significant increase of customers with a poor credit profile may hurt a business financially. Late customer payments usually causes a slow down and tightening of cash flow. In addition, chronically late paying customers squeeze profit margins as financing expenses rise. The lag in payments often makes it necessary to borrow increasingly while awaiting collection.

Uncontrolled growth may even adversely affect operating productivity. Personnel policies and procedures often give way when overloaded by a heavy and unrelenting influx of new employees. Also, because employee ranks suddenly swell, a drop in output may occur due to inadequate training and lack of supervision. These problems in turn lead to abnormally high rate of employee turnover and take a toll on the bottom line.

As you will later learn, the key to healthy growth is setting reasonable limits. New business has to be systematically absorbed and managed in order to achieve best results. Later, I will offer some key insights on different techniques of profitable growth management.

SHARPEN THE MODEL

Along with a marketable product or service, a well-crafted business model is crucial for financial success. This is especially true for entrepreneurial companies with relatively limited capital resources. Relative to business planning and decision-making, their margin for error tends to be extremely slim by comparison to mature businesses. Consequently, a financially sound business model is absolutely imperative.

Perhaps more than any other types of business, general contractors recognize the importance of tailoring their business approach to fit the demands of a particular business opportunity. Most have experienced the shock of learning in the eleventh hour their costs are at risk of exceeding the billable limits on a fixed price contract. Unless the business model is appropriately designed, there is a real possibility of losing money from day one.

A case in point arose early on in my private practice.

A start-up personnel staffing company began to experience severe financial difficulties even though it had landed a large contract with the State. It never seemed to have enough cash to pay its bills.

Even with a potential yearly billing base of $5 million, business debts continued to mount, and the firm began to hemorrhage badly. Average bank balances declined and overdue accounts payables increased. Even when the State agreed to accelerate payment from 30 to 15 days, cash was insufficient to pay outstanding bills. To add fuel to the fire, the company fell behind in payroll tax deposits by more than $150,000.

A detailed analysis of direct labor and overhead costs revealed the pricing structure of the contract was ill-fitted. Under the best conditions, it actually would have cost $5.5 million to fulfill the terms of the deal. Unfortunately, all pertinent administrative labor and related overhead expenses had not been fully factored into the contract price during the bidding process. Consequently, no degree of hard work would overcome the structural loss.[1]

A sound business model is built on effective pricing and cost control. This precept rules out entering into a business proposition based solely on gross dollars rather than the potential for net earnings. Unfortunately, this principle was overlooked by the business referred to above.

Even with sound pricing and cost control, some business models allow for short-term financial losses. For example, start-up busi-

> *No amount of cash infusion will ever be sufficient to remain viable if the business model is flawed.*

nesses by nature usually incur losses during infancy. While ramping up sales revenues, expenses overall may outpace income. Normally, this imbalance will only persist for a relatively short span of time.

Most business models must be continually adjusted and fine-tuned to remain competitive and profitable. As a general rule emerging businesses need an even tighter business model than mature businesses because their capital cushion is usually significantly less.

PRACTICE CRISIS PREVENTION

Surprisingly, many businesses operate in a constant state of crisis. Rather than focus on developing proactive strategies for minimizing close calls and emergencies, they build a greater tolerance for crisis decision-making. After a while, a crisis mentality becomes the dominant culture in these companies.

A crisis mentality focuses more on emergency response than prevention. When operating a business, this could be detrimental because hasty business decisions generally do not allow ample time for advance planning.

A vivid example of a crisis style of management is where a company routinely finds itself racing to borrow money just in time to meet payroll or refinance overdue accounts owed to key suppliers. Unless the cash shortage arises from unforeseeable catastrophic conditions this may be indicative of a crisis mindset. Management should resist accepting real time decisions as the preferred decision making practice.

Needless to say, it is also generally unwise to wait to the midnight hour to attempt to secure capital for investment in operating equipment, business facilities, or plant renovations necessary to support new growth. Funds for capital investment take time to raise. The risk of a business breakdown or partial shut down is greatest when adequate financing is lacking due to last minute requests.

Urgent financing requests generally do not bode well for the quality of management, especially in the eyes of prospective financiers. Entrepreneurs who habitually delay increase the likelihood for rejection. Financiers assume—rightly or wrongly—if efforts to seek financing were pushed back until the eleventh hour, chances are very high some other essential preparations may have gone unaddressed as well. Financiers generally regard management procrastination as a major risk factor.

> *Entrepreneurs may find financiers unwilling to provide funding on a rush basis.*

As will be discussed later in the book, earning a financier's confidence is sometimes very difficult even with a compelling business strategy. Creating the impression that pivotal decisions are routinely made on a crises basis is not helpful. This method of operating suggest chances of business upheaval are exponential.

MAINTAIN CLOSE WATCH

As the lead manager, the CEO can least afford to be laissez-faire about financial monitoring and oversight. Effective oversight demands keeping on top of key facts and figures as they emerge. Moreover, a company's survival and advancement will often depend on how conscientiously the CEO discharges their responsibility.

While it may not be necessary for a CEO to fully understand debits and credits, he or she must understand the story the financial statement numbers tell. Otherwise, they will be unable to truly assess the results of business strategies and tactics. Clearly, without a financial point of reference one would be inclined to overestimate or underestimate a company's strengths and weaknesses. To no surprise, those who spare themselves a regular review of financial statements often wake up to find this company dangerously overextended and swimming in red ink.

Oftentimes, to keep a firm grip, financial operations are broken down into units. Divisions and departments tracked in this manner are commonly referred to as profit centers. To promote better performance, each profit center is usually guided by a simple financial budget. This helps spotlight financial issues along the way in time to make corrections. In order to achieve best performance the complete financial anatomy of your business should always be in plain view.

> *Monitoring your accounts receivables will help identify prevailing cash flow issues in a timely fashion.*

Monitoring inflows and outflows of resources usually takes in-depth analysis. Unfortunately, shorthand methods normally will not suffice. Rarely can you simply rely on monthly bank statements to gauge a drop off in cash flow. Bank statements are not designed to provide a panoramic view of a company's overall financial conditions.

For instance, a concurrent review of accounts receivables might be necessary to identify a drain on cash. Could it be that a disproportionate level of customer receivables may have shifted from 30 to 60 days due to 90 to 120 days due? These insights will only surface from a closer inspection of specific receivables within your customer base.

Entrepreneurs and senior managers have the responsibility to actively monitor the financial well-being of a business. Experienced business people quickly come to discover this takes far more than guess work. Intuitively, you may be tempted to believe your company is operating at a profit; however, a detailed statement of revenues and expenses may quickly refute your profitable supposition.

Conscientious managers recognize the necessity to go the extra mile in order to fully decipher the bottom line and track key factors that affect financial behavior. Losing focus could invite early signs of financial deterioration. By the time they are noticed, the situations may be extremely severe.

The phrase "work smarter, not harder" has no greater application than in financial management and oversight. An entrepreneur with a growing business hardly has any semblance of idle time. It is unimaginable to find one who is able to scrutinize every piece of financial document and piece of paper. Ultimately, you must rely on a well-oiled financial system.

Systematic financial management will be a recurring theme throughout *The Road to MegaSuccess*. To build proficiency in this area, I will closely examine the most common types of financial statements and forecasts, performance measures and business drivers.

Resist Complacency

Suffice it to say, whenever an entrepreneur or key manager becomes visibly satisfied with the status quo it is probably a precursor to financial decline. In business, there is a long held cliché, "you're either working to move up or working to move out." While pursuing the goal to move up, you must actively manage your business.

When times are good, it is very easy to become wedded to a single product, service or customer relationship that has been very rewarding financially. At the time you may not notice the inherent danger in settling on a single source of revenue for livelihood. Needless to say, in this situation a change of circumstance could be a deaf knell. Eisner Communications, a 95-year old advertising firm in Baltimore, Maryland, learned this lesson the hard way.

> According to reports in the Baltimore Sun, US Airways Group, Inc. was Eisner's most prestigious client and accounted for a sizable portion of its annual income. Advertising Age reported US Airways comprised 40 percent of Eisner's revenues in 2004. When US Airways merged with America West, it no longer needed a separate advertising firm and ended the relationship in September 2005.[2]

> As reported in the Sun, despite several large clients and frantic efforts to attract new clients, Eisner could not recover from the loss of US Airways' business. The firm limped along for another year but in November 2006 Eisner closed its doors.

Even a highly successful long-standing business cannot afford becoming over reliant on one source of business. On the contrary, CEOs—with the assistance of key personnel and professional advisors—are wise to regularly evaluate how sources of income are divided.

Companies overly dependent on a limited number of major customers risk business collapse.

In fact, CEOs of major businesses often find it advantageous to lean on a cadre of people from the outside to help judge diversification and other matters. An honest evaluation from people not employed or involved in the business on a daily basis often provide a more objective perspective. They may shed light on the feasibility of your business plan, major financial decision or investment. Many business leaders credit their advisory boards and boards of directors with providing critical feedback at crucial times in their company's development. Later, I will describe the many advantages of appointing an outside support group to act as a think tank.

PLAN FOR SUCCESS

All too common, key decision makers complain about financial difficulties but never seriously take the time to plan for success. Often the missing link between a fledgling business and a highly profitable operation is a comprehensive financial plan. The key to many business turnarounds rests in a simple strategy made up on a series of actions rather than a single solution. Planning provides a treasured opportunity to map out a holistic business strategy.

Most business veterans characterize business plans succinctly into three categories, namely, the best, worst and most likely case scenarios. Under each saga, to improve the odds for success management should play the "what if" game and devise a cogent set of alternative solutions in advance. In essence, planning is a catalyst for creating multiple business strategies.

A select group of powerful planning and diagnostic tools will be on display throughout this book. Moreover, I hope they serve to leverage your financial management skills and ability. Perhaps most important, utilizing these methods should help improve planning and therefore help stimulate profits.

To help with business planning, I will cover the mechanics of the financial forecasting. My position is that a business person should not consider a business plan a meaningful working guide without first completing a financial forecast. A well-documented financial forecast quantifies the owner's vision and tests the reasonableness of the game plan.

At worst financial forecasts are good faith estimates, and at best they are roadmaps to success. Experienced business people think of a financial forecast as a roadmap — a detailed outline of financial milestones. An operating forecast likewise represents a collage of assessments and estimates of production and sales, linked in logical order and covering a designated time period. Although key assumptions in these forecasts may ultimately deviate from reality, a solid set of directions at the outset of a journey is much better than having none at all.

> *A business that does not continually concentrate on repositioning in the marketplace is bound to perish.*

This discussion may be reminiscent of Chapter 1, where I stressed the importance of devoting time to set the right course. Long-term success in business depends on your ability to do just that, strategically position your company. In an environment of changing market conditions and economic pressures this is critical for managing the bottom line.

Sound planning allows highly profitable companies to be proactive. Rarely do major companies decide, for example, to acquire and dispose of operating divisions, introduce and shelve product and service lines, or abruptly hire and fire advertising and marketing agents out of reflex. To the contrary, these options are usually evaluated far in advance. In a pinch, a calculated change in approach may be the only thing that keeps a business afloat financially.

Should proven financial management techniques that work well for major companies be any less productive when used in an entrepreneurial business? The obvious answer, is no. There is no discernable difference between big business and small business when it comes to crafting a financial plan of execution.

Again, operating a profitable business takes the mindset of a marathon runner, constantly plotting time, distance, and position in the pack. To protect his or her advantage, a runner must strategically exert energy and control running speed. In much the same way, an entrepreneur must build financial resiliency and capabilities along with prevailing market conditions.

Before exploring best practices in cash flow planning and management in the next chapter, consider the warning signs in the checklist below to determine if your company could be in danger of any of the pitfalls discussed in this chapter.

CLASSIC PITFALLS—EARLY WARNING SIGNS

1. Profits are decreasing, although sales are increasing.

2. Your company is operating in the red, despite having achieved sales goals.

3. Sufficient cash is never available to meet expenses, despite growth in sales and new accounts.

4. Banks, investors, and other prospective financial partners willingly discuss your financing needs, but are reluctant to invest in your company.

5. Your written business plan garners positive feedback, while your financial assumptions and forecasts receive negative reviews.

6. Incomplete financial documentation detracts from otherwise accurate, reliable, and complete information.

7. The legal structure of your business is questioned routinely by third parties for lack of adequacy and consistency with your business strategy and investor relations.

8. The magnitude of income tax liabilities and insufficient cash to satisfy these obligations regularly surprise you.

9. You are more reliant on your own short-hand calculations of net income and liquidity than on professionally prepared financial statements and ratios.

10. You doubt your business would have real value to a third party if you were to sell it.

NOTABLE REFLECTIONS AT A GLANCE

⤳ Avoid the classic pitfalls that lead to financial collapse.

⤳ Promote profitability through thoughtful financial planning.

⤳ Monitor financial well-being on a regular basis.

⤳ Strengthen the quality of your financial accounting systems to improve decision-making.

⤳ Refrain from becoming overly reliant on a single product, service or customer.

CHAPTER THREE

Map Distance and Direction ... Plot a Positive Cash Flow

| *The Journey* |

Although Matrix has been financially stable for several years, BJ Armstrong still vividly remembers when cash was in short supply. During the third year of operations, Matrix experienced an extended period of negative cash flow from operations. Had it not been for the equity capital he contributed and for a loan provided by a local bank, the company would not have survived. It was not as easy as it sounds, however, because it took BJ several tries to secure the funding.

Because BJ always had a strong relationship with his banker, he expected the bank would approve his initial loan request without hesitation. Sadly, he was mistaken. At that time his company's financial position was a mess, mainly due to the build up and delinquencies of accounts receivable. Many of Matrix's customers were more than 90 days overdue.

The bank was not willing to accept BJ's explanation for the company's tenuous financial condition and turned down his first loan request. For several months BJ had to run Matrix's operations, get the company's receivables under control, and survive with minimal cash. Those were the most stressful months of his career.

With the help of a professional accountant and the switch to on-line banking, BJ brought his cash cycle under control. He learned to monitor how much cash was available to run his business on a daily basis. Eventually BJ's banker grew confident BJ would use a line of credit responsibly and approved Matrix's loan request. BJ knows the key to the turnaround of his business was his attention to managing cash flow.

Great—a prospect you have been chasing for months just asked for your best and final price for a large contract. You sharpen your pencil, but realize you don't have the cash to mobilize the contract if you win the deal. Your challenge for you is finding a way to cover 45 to 60 days of expenses until the first contract payment is received.

Ever had a nightmare in which your business ran out of cash or was in danger of not meeting bi-weekly payroll? Ever think the business was in the black just because cash was in the bank only to discover every dime was owed to creditors? Most seasoned entrepreneurs will answer either or both of these questions "yes."

Entrepreneurs know well the meaning of "juggling cash." Virtually all have at one time or another struggled to maintain a positive cash flow. Managing cash is a survival skill that an entrepreneur has to master to be successful. Accordingly, this chapter focuses on effective cash flow management techniques and solutions.

Chapter Highlights:

- Managing Cash Flow
- Preserving Liquidity
- Tracking Sources And Uses Of Cash
- Understanding Cash Operating Cycles
- Quantifying Cash Requirements

The Cash Realm

Indeed, a merchant's worst nightmare comes with the thought of running out of cash. In the short term, maintaining adequate operating cash is a matter of business survival. An insolvent company is unable to meet its obligations in the ordinary course of business. As a result, it will suffer a shut down or fall off in customer service or production. Sometimes, strained supplier relationships and even bankruptcy might be in store. These are just a few of the serious financial consequences associated with an on-going cash flow deficit.

To the untrained eye a business may appear to be prosperous or even rich, but in reality find itself extremely tight on cash despite the positive value of assets on its books. Typically, cash strapped businesses continually struggle to support their day-to-day need for cash.

Indeed, the first real test of financial vitality is a company's ability to rapidly convert non-cash assets such as customer receivables and inventory into hard cash. In discussing the world renowned financial icon, Warren Buffet, a business executive described Buffett's perspective on cash flow in a US News and World Report article "How to Make Money The Buffett Way" in the following way:

...Buffet makes a conscious attempt to identify companies with a good chance of continuing their success 25 years into the future. "Buffett talks a lot about looking through the front window and not through the rearview mirror," says John Rogers, chairman of Ariel Capital Management in Chicago.

In essence, Buffet peers into the future partly by attempting to calculate the current value of a company's expected future cash flows. It's his way of assessing a company's intrinsic value.[1]

From an investment perspective, cash flow is no less than a reflection of a company's ability to payout earnings to its investors and still have enough cash left over to support future growth. In this sense cash flow is a hard core value indicator. Management also recognizes it takes sufficient cash flow to maintain operating stability.

For cash planning purposes it is useful to think of cash inflows and outflows in the context of a weighted scale. The objective is to keep the scale in balance, or in the best case, assure that cash inflow is greater than outflow. Maintaining the equilibrium requires careful plotting and coordination.

An imbalance in cash flow is typically tied to capitalization, that is, starting or expanding a business without sufficient cash to fund operations during infancy. The risk of a disabling shortfall in cash is greatest in early days, although the same concern will arise even in mature businesses especially as they seek to expand.

Due to factors both within and outside the control of a business owner, managing cash flow can be extremely challenging and stressful at times. Unlike a predictable flow of customer billings and expenses, the actual receipt and consumption of cash tends to be highly erratic and in some circumstances very difficult to plan.

For any business the mere filing of bankruptcy by a major customer can cause cash flow to hemorrhage. From an operational standpoint an unanticipated equipment breakdown, major customer dispute or increase in interest rate on a bank loan will exact heavy blows as well.

An ill-timed expenditure involving the outright purchase of new equipment, a vehicle, building improvements or an advertising campaign also has the potential to deplete precious working capital. Most any type of large outlay, if not duly planned in advance, can cause cash flow to malfunction. Financially savvy businesses do not usually make major commitments of cash without carefully considering their ability to absorb the burden.

An imbalance in cash flow commonly arises due to capitalization that is, starting or expanding a business without sufficient cash to carry on operations during infancy.

The ramifications of a cash flow deficiency can be quite serious. An irreconcilable deficit cash flow could necessitate draconian measures such as selling off equipment, eliminating staff or cutting back in other essential areas. Aside from securing in cash from the outside, the only way to avoid such dire consequences is to realign cash flow. This takes a thorough understanding of techniques for measuring, forecasting and managing cash sources and uses.

IGNITING THE FLOW

Once you enter in the business world, managing cash flow will become a top priority. A positive cash flow normally takes precedent over profitability especially in the infancy stage of a business. Early on, you must be able to find a way to fund expenses in order to allow business initiatives enough time to garner profits. Activities that produce and conversely deplete cash resources during these early stages as well as the normal operating cycle include the following:

CASH INFLOWS	CASH OUTFLOWS
Collections from Customers	Salaries and Wages
Proceeds from Loans	Benefits Costs
Contributions by Owners	Payroll Taxes
Equity Financing from Investors	Production Materials
Property and Equipment Sales	Office Rent
	Business Insurance
	Utilities, including Phones
	Transportation and Travel
	Loan Principal and Interest Payments

Without outside funding virtually every new or expanding business will risk negative cash flow in the short term. Aside from the items listed above, start-up expenditures for items such as advertising, supplies, security deposits, insurance, equipment, renovations, as well as legal and accounting services would deplete resources. Generally these items have to be funded in advance of receiving the first dollar from anticipated customer sales.

At the end of the day, many businesses have to jumpstart cash flow with an injection of cash from the owner's personal funds or with the assistance of outside investors. A business that succeeds in generating profits should eventually be able to repay cash advances and initial investments. The art of growing profits will be addressed in depth in Chapter 4.

Before seeking outside funding you should first estimate the size and source of any projected cash deficits. Differentiating between the need to cover normal operating expenses such as rent and payroll in contrast to capital items as in investment in equipment is a prerequisite for deciding the best approach to fulfill cash requirements.

When starting a new business or expanding an existing one, a cash flow deficit for several months or years may be considered normal while the level of customer collections catches up to the rate of disbursements. Suffice it to say, business owners should attempt to gauge the gap in advance. This is a prerequisite that depends on reliably forecasting financing requirements. A full discussion of growth financing will be covered in Chapter 7.

Outside funding is a must when your appetite for cash is not fulfilled from the sale of goods and services.

At the cornerstone of sound cash flow planning is a concept known as "coverage ." Coverage focuses on sufficient cash available to cover anticipated expenditures at just the right time. Without adequate cash coverage , key aspects of your business plan may have to be drastically modified or put on hold.

Gauging the adequacy of cash flow coverage begins with mapping your cash flow DNA. Two businesses—retail operations and government contracting companies—highlight the range of possibilities. The source of cash flow for retail is mostly over the counter sale, an immediate event. In contrast, a government contracting company is usually required to perform work and then submit to inspection, audit and regulatory approval before receiving payment. The extent of cash coverage necessary in these polar opposite situations will naturally vary substantially.

Far different coverage in cash will also be necessary for businesses engaged in research and development. They usually have substantial "front loaded" cash coverage requirements triggered operating expenses that must be incurred. The lag between expenditures and cash from sales may be months or even years while a product is under development. In the latter case, such companies will have to place a much greater reliance on outside funding at the beginning of a business undertaking. Due to a lengthy product rollout, any form of outside funding that will require short-term repayment may have to be ruled out.

Understanding the operating cycle of a business is also key to structuring funding. For instance, the timeline from sales billings, receiving cash and paying vendors is known as the operating cycle. Fortunately, most entrepreneurial companies have an operating cycle that falls between the retail and research development business models described earlier. The average company experiences a 30 to 60 day lag between billings and collections and has a comparable timeline for payment of its bills.

CRITICAL NEEDS ASSESSMENT

Most business decisions impact cash directly or indirectly. Accordingly, hurried and impulsive decisions may prove to be disastrous. To avoid costly missteps the impact on cash flow should always be carefully evaluated prior to committing to any major expenditure of funds.

From the outset, it is wise to take time to take a full review of your cash position. This requires examining the total array of foreseeable sources and uses of cash over the next week, month, and quarter. .

To identify critical needs, a business must plan ahead. A thorough assessment of the future serves to reveal all anticipated sources and uses of cash funds. It will also delineate timing. While transactions such as loan payments along with income and payroll taxes are generally subject to fixed payment dates, the scheduling of other activities may be adapted. Clearly, the best point to perform the analysis is before operations for the year shift into full swing.

Cash may be conserved by adjusting the timing of future purchases of equipment, payment of bonuses, or debt pay off.

The following summary is offered as a simple guide for identifying areas of need that cannot be ignored in assessing cash flow:

PERSONNEL:

- Employee salaries, wages and benefits
- Employee incentives and bonuses
- Outside employee training

OPERATING CASH:

- Vendor and supplier credit obligations
- Contractual debt payments
- Business growth and expansion initiatives

CONTINGENCIES:

- Rainy day fund for unexpected emergencies
- Reserves to cover insurance deductibles

- Funds to replace aging equipment and facilities

FINANCING:

- Short term debts such as lines of credit
- Long term loans such as mortgages

MASSAGING THE CYCLE

Most business owners feel it is in their best interest to perpetually hunt for opportunities to accelerate cash flow from operations. However, even with a diligent effort rarely will the timing of cash disbursements and receipts match up perfectly. Coming close to alignment would feel like Utopia for most entrepreneurs. The practical objective is to produce incremental improvements that make the cash operating cycle more efficient.

A graphical depiction of the cash flow cycle in what might be considered perfect alignment versus imperfect alignment is shown below:

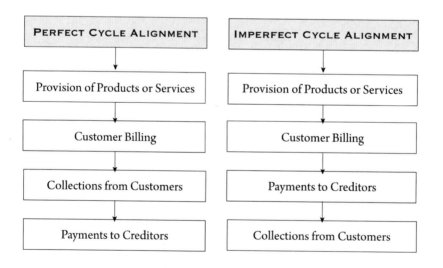

Unfortunately, very few businesses enjoy the luxury of a perfect cycle alignment. Practically speaking, it is not feasible to affect the timing of certain activities. Nevertheless, positive change is measured wherever possible no matter how slight. In aggregate, the effect could make the difference in maintaining a positive cash balance.

> *It is virtually impossible to maintain the inflow and outflow of cash in perfect harmony.*

Tweaking financial policies and practices in order to achieve tighter cash flow alignment should be an ongoing process. For instance, rather than bill or invoice customers bi-monthly consider weekly invoicing. Likewise, as opposed to adhoc purchasing, delay inventory and supply purchases nearer to actual usage. Each of these tactics has the potential to tighten the operating cycle.

Discretion in setting customer payment terms is also a powerful cash lever. Management is wise to scrutinize standard customer billing and credit policies on a regular basis and make appropriate modifications. For example, to the extent customer accounts can be converted faster from billing to collection, payment in advance or progress payments, the length of the normal operating cycle should be shortened. In essence, payment terms should be tailored to speed the flow of collections whenever possible.

Even relatively minor tweaks in contractual terms stand to yield significant benefits toward positive cash flow . Borrowers normally have an opportunity to select monthly payment due dates in connection with bank loans and other debts. Choosing a date at the beginning, middle or end of the month may have major cash flow implications. Ideally, a payment schedule should be consistent with the time of month when cash collections are at their highest. Synchronizing regular payments according to the pattern of cash receipts helps keep cash flow in balance.

Solving cash flow challenges starts with a detailed diagram of activities involving cash inflows and outflows.

A thorough study of the operating cycle may reveal many other opportunities to energize cash flow. Leaks may be detected in the progression from customer order, requisition, deployment of labor, shipping, billing to collection. Charting the processing sequence may help to pinpoint both leakages and blockages. Most important, business managers must never assume there is no room for improvement.

Shortening the normal lag between billings and collections is an overriding objective in any strategy to improve cash efficiency. Many pertinent factors are within management control.

RELIEVING THE PRESSURE

Major anticipated cash flow disruptions must be counter-balanced, either internally or externally. Operating procedures involving tightening customer credit policies that affect cash may not always correct the problem. Sometimes securing external resources is the only answer.

Cash flow relief is usually found in various adjustments to daily routines and business practices.

However, external financing should not necessarily be the first avenue taken to cure a major cash flow squeeze. On the contrary, consideration should be given to adjusting the timing of planned activity. For example, delaying equipment purchases and payment of bonuses, or renegotiating payment terms on debt may relieve stress on cash flow. When operating cash is in short supply, these types of transactional adjustments should be studied. Many possible solutions

> *Meeting cash management objectives requires well trained staff to administer accounts receivable.*

work best in combination rather than as a single prescription.

For the most part, cash flow remedies fall under two basic categories: (1) those that minimize collection float (the period between when you issue and invoice and receive payment); and (2) those that maximize disbursement float (the period between when you incur an expense and when you pay for it). Examples of these techniques are outlined below:

MINIMIZE COLLECTION LAG:

- Tighten customer payment terms, i.e., from 45 to 30 days
- Tighten credit granting by securing D&B and credit references
- Strengthen collection procedures for delinquent accounts with reminders and demand letters
- Offer customer incentives such as a 2% discount for early payment
- Improve product quality thus reducing sales returns

MAXIMIZE DISBURSEMENT FLOAT:

- Control timing of inventory purchases to coincide with the timing of actual usage

- Authorize vendor payments no earlier than the due date
- Minimize operating expenses to reduce burden on cash flow
- Search for suppliers who offer more lenient payment terms

CEOs also should be on guard for cash flow inefficiencies tied to their management practices. For example, often due to limited staff in entrepreneurial businesses many arbitrarily select just and employee to be in charge of billings and collections. This could compound collection delays because assigned personal lack the knowledge and organizational skills necessary to administer accounts receivable efficiently.

Lax supervision and oversight of billing and collection functions is the Achilles Heal of many large and small companies. Deficiencies extend from a lack of formal follow-up procedures regarding delinquent paying customers, delay in circulating payment reminders, to unreasonable delay in correcting routine billing errors. These shortcomings will deal a heavy blow to cash flow. Very often the cure to chronic cash flow struggles lie in weeding out these practices.

Telltale signs that turbulent cash flow is on the horizon may include the following:

- Customer accounts 60 and 90 days overdue
- Excessive build up in merchandise held in stock for resale
- Growing overdue balances owed to supplies and other creditors
- Payroll and sales tax deposit penalty assessments
- Overdue lease and mortgage payments
- Arrears on bank loan payments

Banking On It

Cash flow may be stimulated methodically by investing bank deposits. Investing available funds as soon as possible and for as long as possible could provide an income stream. This is the ultimate goal of effective cash management.

Beyond operational and policy issues cash management requires making your money work for you at all times. Accordingly, a business should concentrate on accelerating the transfer of funds to interest bearing accounts. They should rarely be parked in a non-interest bearing position.

Entrepreneurs often overlook cash management services, assuming they are only available to big businesses. Do not make this mistake. Most commercial banks offer a host of cash management options to customers of all sizes.

Banks may not always aggressively market their cash management services customer-wide because from an economic perspective these programs may be less profitable for them. Entrepreneurs should be proactive. It is very rare to find a highly successful business that does not take full advantage of their bank's cash management resources. Typically, these services center around overnight investing, lock box processing and other deposit functions.

Common cash management support to look for includes:

PROCESSING:

- **Lockbox**—Lets the bank perform your high-volume deposit processing.

- **Imaging/CD-Rom Storage**—Eliminates the need for canceled check by providing permanent electronic file of all cleared checks.

- **Automated Clearinghouse (ACH) Payments**—Inexpensive way to initiate future dated electronic payments to your vendors; includes direct deposit payroll.

MONITORING:

- **Daily Transaction Log**—Shows all transactions cleared the previous day; allows for daily reconciliation.

- **Zero Balance Accounts**—Allows all sub-account balances at one bank to be swept into a master account for investing purposes.

INVESTING:

- **Remote Deposit**—Scans checks received for deposit as if there was a physical deposit at the bank.

- **Overnight Sweeps**—Investment of available funds each night.

- **Concentration Account**—Automatically concentrates funds available in multiple accounts at multiple banks into lead bank for investment.

SAFEGUARDING:

- **Positive Pay**—All checks written on your account first are compared to the file to mitigate the risk of forged checks.

- **Balance Reporting**—Allows you to see available and uncollected balances immediately.

FORECASTING CASH FLOW

Reliably forecasting cash flow is a strategic advantage. This critical skill not only helps to smooth out peaks and valleys but quantify the precise amount of financing needed from outside sources. Because operating conditions that impact cash flow usually change on a daily basis, cash forecasts should be updated routinely.

Financial experts agree the best way to protect a positive cash flow in a tight economy is by devising cash flow strategies under different scenarios. A complete analysis requires a breakdown of cash flow assumptions by week, month, and quarter. A full discussion of budget methods is contained in Chapter 8. Nevertheless, it is reasonable to assume most business budgets are subject to a variety of uncertainties that should not be ignored.

> *Entrepreneurs often overlook the cash management services offered by banks, assuming they are only for businesses that generate substantial cash. Do not make this mistake.*

> *The only way to maintain a positive cash flow in a tight economy is with a cash flow projection outlining anticipated flow of collections and payments.*

In order to master forecasting, entrepreneurs must resist the temptation to pass on preparation of a cash flow projection to their accountants. A CEOs' thoughtful insights and expression of intentions are crucial to development of the projection. Crunching numbers is really the easy part of the process and lends itself to delegation. On the other hand, formulating growth, financing and investing assumptions requires direct participation at the executive level. Investors and bankers expect an entrepreneur and CEO to be the primary architect of the projection.

For illustrative purposes, assume Potomac Technologies (one of the companies in the case study) decides to open a "New Division." In connection with this business initiative Potomac decides to prepare a projection to quantify the cash funding requirements for the first two months of operations. The sample analysis might appear as follows:

NEW DIVISION POTOMAC, LLC		
CASH FLOW PROJECTION	MONTH 1	MONTH 2
Beginning Cash in Bank	$100,000	$175,550
Loan Proceeds	300,000	0
Cash Collections from Customers	0	75,000
Cash Disbursements for Labor	(224,500)	(196,500)
Net Cash Available for Debt Service	$175,500	$54,000

As a manager assigned to oversee New Division, what response would you provide to the following questions?

a. Without a $300,000 loan, would New Division have a positive cash balance at the end of month one?

b. Was the assumed initial $100,000 of cash in bank critical in month two?

c. New Division's customers will be invoiced "30 days net." The average collections will be, 50 percent of customers made timely and 50 percent within 60 days. Assuming sales of $15,000 in month one, in what time period and in what amount should cash collections be projected for months one, two and three?

d. If New Division is obligated to pay 100 percent of its advertising in month one, should the entire annual expense be factored into the cash flow projection in month one or spread evenly over twelve months?

e. By the end of the second month will New Division have enough cash to completely repay the $300,000 loan?

Upon reflection, would you agree with the following statements?

a. A loan of approximately $300,000 will be critical during the first month of operation.

b. An initial $100,000 cash in the bank from Potomac is essential for a positive cash position by the end of month two.

c. The projection of cash from customer collections should be spread over the anticipated period of collection. In this case, $150,000 of sales in month one is expected to be received incrementally, 50 percent or $75,000 in month two, and 50 percent or $75,000 in month three.

d. Because advertising is required to be paid in advance, costs should be reflected as an expenditure in month one.

e. New Division will not be in a position to repay the loan of $300,000 in full by the end of the second month.

In practice, a cash flow projection would typically offer more detail than the sample model featured. Among other things, a summary of underlying operating assumptions, itemized line items for cash receipts and expenditures; and the cash flow projection would cover at least twelve months. An outline of the basic preparation mechanics is provided below.

PROJECTING CASH FLOW—STEP BY STEP:

1. Estimate monthly sales and associated billings. The estimate should reflect past sales histories, current market assessment and marketing plans. Document basis for estimates.

2. Estimate average number of days between sales and collections. This should take into account customer payment terms, past payment history and other pertinent factors. Document assumptions.

3. Convert monthly sales into monthly cash equivalents based on payment assumptions.

4. Budget direct expenses for cost of direct labor and inventory. Direct expenses generally vary with changes in sales revenue. Delineate payment via same month of sale, thirty (30) days or sixty (60) days. Document assumptions.

5. Identify fixed operating expenses payable each month. Document assumptions.

6. Account for cash outlays for start-up costs and investments in plant and equipment. List any special receipts such as proceeds from a loan or sale of equipment.

7. Compute the net cash balance at the end of each month, and transfer this figure forward as beginning cash for the next month.

NOTABLE REFLECTIONS AT A GLANCE

→ Efficient management of the operating cycle improves cash flow.

→ Controlling the timing of customer collections, vendor disbursements and/or financing is key to effective management of cash flow.

→ A cash flow projection diagrams anticipated sources and uses of cash.

→ Internal business practices must be cash efficient.

→ Tap into your bank's cash management services to maximize returns.

→ For emerging and growing businesses, Cash is King!

CHAPTER FOUR

Adopt the Golden Rule ... "Net" Trumps "Gross"

| *The Journey* |

Several days after reuniting with BJ, Taylor contacted a manufacturer of computer chips to investigate the possibility of Potomac becoming one of its regional product distributors. She believes an exclusive marketing arrangement could be a highly profitable undertaking. Conceivably, Potomac would be in position to achieve two of its main business objectives: diversification and growth. However, such a deal would most likely require Potomac to invest in expanded facilities and hire more people.

Taylor mentioned the distribution opportunity to her sales manager, Eileen Jones. They spent an afternoon pondering its sales potential but were unable to reach a decision. Taylor fears competition would be too strong to generate enough sales to make a profit. In the end they were left with a fundamental unanswered question, what level of sales will it take to breakeven?

Congratulations, entrepreneur! You have launched a highly successful marketing campaign and sales are increasing. Your business is on its way to meeting current financial objectives.

OR IS IT?

Can it be sales are increasing but profits are decreasing? Is a seemingly lucrative deal about to bring you to the brink of financial disaster? Are you questioning whether a new business product or service will make money? Are you staying up late at night debating whether your business will end the year in the black or in the red?

Profit—or the lack of it—goes directly to the heart and soul of any business. In the long term, profit is the key to survival. To become financially stable you must have a viable profit model.

Ideally, your profit model should allow your company to generate some margin of profit on virtually every sale. In essence, you should be in position to make more money from the sale of a widget than it cost to produce. A viable profit strategy aims to transfer profit margins to the bottom line after paying operating expenses. Offsetting expense comes in the form of wages, salaries, office rent, advertising, insurance, and other outlays normally associated with running a business.

If you are among the innumerable entrepreneurs and managers struggling to profitably manage the bottom line, this chapter is a must-read.

CHAPTER HIGHLIGHTS:

→ Breaking Even

→ Profit Modeling

+ Planning for Profit

+ Strategic Pricing

CONQUERING "BREAK EVEN"

Determining breakeven performance will provide answers to many strategic business questions. Should the company execute or pass up a commercial contract? Could prices be raised or lowered without sacrificing earnings? What level of sales will it take to increase earnings by 10%, 15%, or 20%? Answers to these questions are vital to effective profit management and growth.

The critical threshold for sales of products and services is the breakeven point. At breakeven revenues from sales match operating expenses. Any revenue in excess of this threshold will contribute to what is interchangeably referred to as net income, profit or earnings.

Financially speaking it would be unwise for a business to sell a product or service below cost except for promotional reasons. Otherwise, with each sale a business will lose money with each sale.

Envision the inverse pricing structure shown below:

Sales Price per Unit	$30
Cost per Unit	32
Negative Profit Margin per Unit	($ 2)

Obviously, it would be financially counterproductive to promote a product or service that does not have the potential to generate a positive margin. In the example above the product would essentially lose $2 on each sale even before considering basic operating and administrative expenses.

Breakeven straightforwardly asks: How much product or service do I have to sell to cover expected operating expenses? The success or failure of a business venture will depend on both knowing and reaching the breakeven point.

> *Breakeven straight forwardly asks: How much product or service do I have to sell to cover expected operating expenses?*

Solving for breakeven requires several steps. First, business expenses have to be classified either as direct or indirect. The distinction between direct and indirect is a function of whether the specific expense involved increases or decreases whenever sales volume rises and falls. Those expenses that fluctuate with sales activity are generally grouped as direct expenses. For most companies, labor and material make up the lion's share of direct expenses.

Expenses that behave different in a more static sense than direct expenses are simply classified as indirect. Characteristically indirect or fixed expenses remain mostly flat even while sales levels rise and fall. Most often items such as officers' compensation, administrative salaries, insurance, office rent, supplies, travel, and other costs necessary to support production or delivery of services fall in this category. The importance of distinguishing direct and indirect expenses will become more evident as we explore several applications of the breakeven model.

For practical context, assume the mythical Potomac Technologies is faced with the following dilemma:

For Potomac Technologies to sign on as a wholesale distributor of computer chips the company will need to take on additional fixed expenses—administrative salaries, office rent, utilities, travel, and professional and other indirect expenses totaling $425,000. Potomac's direct cost per computer chip will be $20. The suggested retail selling price is $30 per chip. Under this pricing and cost model, what is Taylor's breakeven point measured in the number of units and sales dollars?

FIGURING BREAKEVEN

1. **Breakeven Units:**

   - Net Profit = Sales Price – Direct Expense

   - Breakeven Point (Units) = Indirect Expenses ÷ Net Profit

2. **Breakeven Sales:**

   - Net Profit % = Net Profit ÷ Sales Price

   - Breakeven Point (Sales Dollars) = Indirect Expenses ÷ Net Profit %

Based on the analysis highlighted Potomac's prospective new opportunity will not be financially viable until unit sales reach 42,500 units. In essence, it will take selling this minimum number of units in order to achieve breakeven. For decision makers it is critically important to know that until business cracks this sales level it will operate in the red.

PRELIMINARY STEP		FINAL STEP	
BREAKEVEN IN UNITS			
Sales Price	$30	Indirect Expense	$425,000
-Direct Expense	20	÷ Net Profit	10
Net Profit	$10	Breakeven Units	42,500
BREAKEVEN SALES DOLLARS			
Net Profit	$10	Indirect Expense	$425,000
÷ Sales Price	30	÷ Net Profit	33%
Net Profit %	33%	Breakeven Sales	$1,287,878

TAILORING THE SOLUTION

By now, it should be clear that calculating your breakeven point is the first major milestone on the road to increasing profitability. Essentially, breakeven pinpoints a specific target benchmark for both sales and expenses. Mastering the technique offers immediate benefit both financially and operationally.

By dissecting the revenue and expense components of your business operation and separating them into a simple equation, it is much easier to both devise and modify a plan for profit. Furthermore, the breakeven model makes it much simpler to discern whether a new deal, product or investment under consideration will offer a realistic prospect of profit.

Companies express breakeven in different ways depending on line of business. These options include units sold, ticket sales, repeat orders and other quantifiable activities. For example, many service providers, such as consultants, lawyers, accountants, and engineers, compute breakeven based on billable hours. An illustration of breakeven technique found in these businesses is below:

$$\text{Breakeven Billable Hours} = \text{Overhead/Indirect Costs} \div \text{Net Profit per Hour}$$

The breakeven model is highly adaptable to practically any business. Several notable specialized industry applications are highlighted below:

- Product and merchandising companies, such as retail and wholesale operations, express breakeven in sales dollars.

- Construction companies typically spread breakeven over a certain number of anticipated construction projects.

- Companies that supply transportation services such as airlines, quantify breakeven based on average daily passengers or passenger miles.

- Healthcare services routinely measure breakeven based on a certain level of patient visits.

The breakeven calculation provides the building blocks for a profitable operation. It serves two distinct purposes: (1) to sufficiently describe management's vision of how the company plans to generate income; and (2) to establish specific financial benchmarks for making money. On the one hand, it is important to remember that the confidence you accord to these parameters should depend on the reliability of key assumptions about each variable and not just the result itself.

The value of breakeven forecasts, largely depends on how well you gauge expected future revenues as well as costs. If the market will not support the assumed sales price, the estimate could be very misleading. To firm up price estimates a market study or survey could be necessary.

On the other hand, "tag along expense items" must not be overlooked in estimating direct and indirect expenses. For instance, you will not want to ignore employer taxes, shipping and delivery or any

> *When fully outlined, the profit model is the roadmap for converting gross sales into bottom-line profit.*

other expense that may not clearly stand out or be readily apparent. In addition, the forecast should take into account widespread economic changes that may affect the market. Especially in volatile economic times, price adjustments, rate increases, and inflation have to be accounted for. Finally, your breakeven should contain a plan A and B, consisting of a best case and worst case scenario.

Even with conservative allowances, a business owner should continually update the projection based on actual experience. In fact, you should assume the targets established will need to be adjusted periodically.

Banks and other prospective financiers are keenly interested in management's updated outlook based on their projections. They will want to be informed about the rationale behind revised estimates as well as the underlying facts. This type of feedback can either build or destroy investor confidence. Therefore, your breakeven calculation should be designed to enable a prospective financier to draw their own conclusion about the feasibility of the business model. Even a business' tax advisor will have an interest in financial estimates and details behind the plan to get there.

Finally, in tweaking a breakeven forecast, past experience can also be very helpful. Right or wrong, most outsiders will consider historical financial data as their main reference point when evaluating your financial forecasts.

RUNNING THE OFFENSE

Once your company reaches breakeven, net profit on each additional unit sold should flow right to the bottom line. In order to produce maximum earnings, it is important to specify monthly, quarterly and yearly targets relative to sales, profit margin and expenses. No matter the industry, size, or structure, breakeven planning performed in this manner provides a convenient way to promote greater productivity and profitability.

No matter the industry, size, or structure, breakeven planning offers a convenient way to promote greater productivity and profitability.

When deciding how high to set the bar, entrepreneurs frequently ask, "At what level of revenue will the company achieve a profit of X?" To find the answer, the profit or income target has to simply be factored into the breakeven calculation as another component of fixed expense. This allows desired profit to fit neatly into the breakeven equation. Using Potomac's proposed new venture for reference, the following is a chart that would assist Potomac in profit planning:

ALTERNATIVE PROFIT SCENARIOS

PROFIT OBJECTIVE	PRELIMINARY STEPS	FINAL STEPS
$100,000	Fixed Expense $425,000 + Target Profit $100,000 Combined Total $525,000	Combined Total $525,000 ÷ Net Profit $ 10 52,500 units
$500,000	Fixed Expense $425,000 + Target Profit $500,000 Combined Total $925,000	Combined Total $925,000 ÷ Net Profit $10 92,500 units

Based on the analysis, Potomac would need to sell at least 52,500 units to generate a net income of $100,000. On the other hand, the company needs to sell 92,500 units to achieve a profit of $500,000. In the real business world, Potomac would also be wise to consider sales demand along with its operating and financing capacity. The latter will be covered in depth later in the book.

Strategically, profit building requires business owners to look to the incremental gain contributed from each additional sale after exceeding breakeven. A grid or step ladder depicting the cumulative gain at various levels may provide necessary guidance for deciding whether to expand and invest in new equipment and facilities. A sample breakdown for Potomac's new venture might appear as follows:

> *Entrepreneurs frequently ask, "At what level of revenue will the company achieve a profit of X?"*

FINANCIAL BENCHMARKS							
UNIT SALES	−	BREAK-EVEN UNITS	=	UNITS @ NET PROFIT	=	NET INCOME
52,500	−	42,500	=	10,000 @ $10	=	$100,000
62,500	−	42,500	=	20,000 @ $10	=	$200,000
72,500	−	42,500	=	30,000 @ $10	=	$300,000
82,500	−	42,500	=	40,000 @ $10	=	$400,000
92,500	−	42,500	=	50,000 @ $10	=	$500,000

The chart shown above is germane to profit planning. First, it focuses attention on incremental gains based on average profit margin of $10 on each sale. Secondly, it forecasts cumulative net income. Understanding these dynamics is essential when devising a comprehensive business plan.

As a practical matter, breakeven is often used within a company to budget profit between various operating groups and units. It can serve to promote healthy competition within the business. In essence, breakeven may be used to encourage each division or unit to elevate their performance. Finally, breakeven will be a guide for setting benchmarks by product line, region or subsidiary.

Ordinarily, the CEO should have the final say on how to fine tune the breakeven application. Ultimately, they will be accountable for good and bad results. As such, CEOs are either widely acclaimed or severely criticized. With so many estimates involving a high degree of uncertainty decision makers must always be totally engaged and prepared to make real time adjustments.

IMPROVISE TO MAXIMIZE

At the end of the day, the hallmark of a financially progressive business is an ability to maintain superior financial performance even when economic conditions change. Perseverance requires sound planning as well as efficient management of revenues and expenses. The solid approach you relied on to yield high returns yesterday may not be in vogue tomorrow. Accordingly, CEOs have to be adept at improvising on the run.

A look at even some of the most profitable businesses confirms the necessity for innovation in order to grow profits.

> Parker Hannifin Corp., a manufacturer of precision-engineered motion and control systems, offers a unique look at how a comprehensive understanding of breakeven can lead to better pricing decisions and greater profitability. As reported in the Wall Street Journal, Parker's CEO Donald Washkewicz eliminated the 89-year-old company's historic pricing policies in favor of "perfect prices." The goal was to use strategic pricing levels to decrease breakeven volumes and increase profitability.

> Parker produces approximately 800,000 products for clients in a wide array of industries, including aerospace, transportation, power generation and the military. Revenues reached $9.4 billion in 2006.

As reported in the Journal, the company traditionally priced all of its products using the same formula. "Company managers would calculate how much it cost to make and deliver each product and add a flat percentage on top, usually aiming for about 35%." Similar pricing models are used by companies throughout the world.

While this pricing approach is relatively simple, it runs the risk of leaving money on the table. It focuses exclusively on cost, but does not take into account the value of Parker's products to its clients. In contrast, strategic pricing emphasizes what customers are willing to pay for products, taking into account their uniqueness, convenience and competition.

Parker sought to divide its products into four categories, from high-volume commodities to highly specialized items. Prices of most commodity products were kept stable, while prices of more unique and customized products were increased. Price increases were as high 60%, with an average increase of 5%. Even a few prices were decreased.

By increasing the prices of items for which the market is least cost sensitive – roughly one-third of the total—Parker has decreased the breakeven volume of several product lines. This pricing strategy also enables the company to benefit from manufacturing improvements and efficiencies, rather than foregoing potential earnings.

Washkewicz reports the strategic pricing initiative has been very successful.

...the company says its new pricing approach boosted operating income by $200 million since 2002. That helped Parker's net income soar to $673 million last year from $130 million in

2002. Now the company's return on invested capital has risen from 7% in 2002 to 21% in 2006 ... [1]

In the Parker case, simple changes in the company's pricing technique did indeed increase profit margins, lower breakeven and thereby yield a handsome boost to the bottom line. Renewed profit strategies often come in the form of more efficient pricing, lowering direct expenses and cutting back on indirect expenses. As suggested earlier, these upgrades must be made continually because the economic landscape of every business and the economy at large is constantly changing.

THE CEO'S MESSAGE

Maximizing profit requires more than a mathematical formula. The formal CEO's message to the company often makes a real difference, especially when specific financial goals are embraced and fully understood by the rank and file.

A CEO like a coach must create a financial playbook that every member of the team will be able to comprehend. At a bare minimum, the playbook should succinctly map targeted sales performance, spending limitations and earnings projections. The goal is to get everyone on the same page from day one. A simple game plan might resemble the matrix illustrated on the following page.

> *A CEO like a coach must create a financial playbook that every member of the team will be able to comprehend.*

BUSINESS OBJECTIVE	FINANCIAL PERFORMANCE GOAL	TIME PERIOD		
		YEAR 1	YEAR 2	YEAR 3
GROWTH	$ Sales	$5,000K	$5,250K	$5,565K
	% of Sales Growth	4%	5%	6%
MARGINS	Net Profit % of Sales	43%	45%	47%
	Cost Good Sold % of Sales	57%	55%	53%
FINANCIAL RETURN	Net Income	$431K	$450K	$500K
	Net Income % of Sales	9%	9%	9%
QUALITY ASSURANCE	Purchase Return % of Sales	0.5%	0.5%	0.5%
	Sale Return % of Sales	2%	2%	1%
HUMAN RESOURCES	Salaries % of Sales	12%	13%	14%
	Employee Benefit % of Salaries	20%	20%	20%
DISTRIBUTION OF EARNINGS	$ Dividend (Earnings) Payout	$100K	$150K	$200K
	Dividends % of Net Income	23%	33%	40%

The CEO's outlook on future financial performance sets the stage for profitable performance. However, even the most carefully crafted formula alone will not do the trick. The vision should be outlined in a logical framework in order to promote a unified work effort. Indeed, a clearly articulated agenda will serve to synchronize marketing campaigns, hiring decisions, equipment purchases, enhancements in infrastructure and other business decisions.

On an annual basis, regardless of business size it's CEO should lay out a financial blueprint that their management team will be expected to follow. Most important, the synopsis should answer the following questions:

- What is the expected revenue in years one through three?

- What is the profitability target over the next three years?

- What overall profit margin level is necessary for the company to achieve its financial objectives?

- What resources will be acquired and made available to facilitate expected performance?

The opportunity to expound on specific financial goals and key success measures should be maximized to build momentum. Subordinates should be guided to facilitate the development of necessary internal processes and policies over sales, production, budgets and even, performance appraisals. It is generally recognized that a CEO's vision is much easier to activate when people within the organization fully understand quantifiable goals and objectives.

NOTABLE REFLECTIONS AT A GLANCE

→ Breakeven constitutes a barometer for business management.

→ Simple profit-modeling estimates direct and indirect expenses in computing margins.

→ Breakeven drives development of performance goals and standards.

→ Breakeven models must be customized to business and industry.

→ Net always trumps Gross.

CHAPTER FIVE

Perform A Reality Check...
Examine Your Financials

| *The Journey* |

Taylor Made has good news: Potomac is being considered for several large contracts. Each offers the potential for a handsome financial return. In anticipation of the incurring startup expenditures for additional staff and equipment Taylor pulls out Potomac's most recent financial statements. In the course of the review, she realizes all the cash in bank is fully spoken for. Most of it will be needed to pay outstanding supplier invoices. However, accounts receivable are fully collected Potomac should be able to spare some extra cash to fund most necessary contract startup expenses.

Taylor was encouraged that her company's income statement reflected positive earnings for the most recent year. However, her elation was tempered by the fact there has been no significant increase in sales revenues for the past two years. Last year, in an attempt to spark sales growth, Taylor authorized purchase of new equipment to enhance the company's operating capacity. She wonders how the investment in equipment will show up on Potomac's statement of cash flow and balance sheet.

In anticipation of the new contracts Taylor requested a meeting with the company's banker, Steve Pool. She thought it would be wise to have a discussion about the possible need for short-term funding. However, Steve requested Taylor supply her company's most recent financial statements in advance of their meeting. Realizing that she will have to discuss Potomac's financial statements with Steve outside the presence of her accountant causes Taylor to a panic.

We've all heard the adage, "A picture is worth a thousand words." Well, ultimately a high resolution picture of the financial profile of your business is worth thousands of words! A high resolution picture typically is presented in the form of financial statements. In this sense, financial statements are like a set of medical x-rays.

Outsiders rarely "take your word for it" when evaluating your company's financial status. Validation comes from the reliability and completeness of your business' financial statements. Whether you are attempting to secure a business loan, commercial mortgage, vendor credit, or investor capital, the content and quality of your financial statements will be scrutinized. The story they tell has many chapters –including your profitability, assets, debts and equity – just to name a few. Your company's financial statements also indicate the strength of your company's financial infrastructure. From an outsider's perspective a company that lacks the ability to produce financial statements may also lack the capacity to profitably manage invested funds.

Financial statements are designed to benefit your business in two fundamental ways. First, financial statements track the flow of financial resources. Secondly, they provide a way to keep score of financial performance. Accordingly, financial statements are critical for sound management. Also, they provide answers to questions typically raised by investors, bankers and other interested third parties.

Do you feel uncomfortable navigating between different financial statements? Do you have difficulty locating critical financial information about your business? Are you overly dependent on your accountant to interpret the meaning of the financial data? Have you ever been shocked by unfavorable conclusions reached by a potential investor about the financial strengths and weakness of your business? If you answered yes to any of these questions this chapter should be especially helpful. It speaks to the entrepreneur who experiences anxiety, frustration or confusion when attempting to apply and interpret conventional financial statements.

CHAPTER HIGHLIGHTS:

→ Fundamentals of Financial Statements

→ Financial Statement Applications and Uses

→ Needs of Investors and Bankers

→ Management Guides for Interpretation

→ Analytical Insights

INSIDE THE LINES

Because they are verifiable by audit, financial statements play a vital role in business management and finance. They help to gauge the true financial condition and past performance of a business enterprise. In essence, financial statements provide a detailed photograph of the financial history and current status of a business.

The phrase "financial statements" normally refers to three conventional report types: Income Statement, Balance Sheet and Cash Flow Statement. The quantitative financial information presented by each speaks to a specific area of business up keep and maintenance. Collectively, financial statements also offer a snapshot of a company's financial anatomy.

The title ascribed to each financial statement explains its respective purpose and application. Still, it may be helpful to think about each statement in everyday terms. For instance, CEOs tend to be very concerned with bottom line earnings (income statement), cash generated (cash flow statement) and net worth (balance sheet). The bare bones of each financial statement are highlighted below

Income Statement	Measures profitability—revenues from sales less costs of products or services and any other expenses necessary to operate the business. Normally covers a month, quarter, or year.
Cash Flow Statement	Breakdown of cash activity—lists all sources and uses of cash whether tied to operations, capital infusions or loans. Report captures activity during a month, quarter or year.
Balance Sheet	Addresses liquidity and net changes in worth—reports detailed company assets, liabilities and equity. Pinpoints financial status at the end of a month, quarter or year.

Financial statements equate to a personal medical evaluation. Just as a spot on an x-ray may indicate a health concern, financial statements highlight unusual patterns. Items valued in financial statements range from assets, liabilities, capital, revenues and expenses to cash proceeds from assets sales, loans and contributed capital.

From a business owner's perspective financial statements provide a periodic report card highlighting financial progress as well as short-comings. They also serve as a handy guide for making financial decisions. With these applications in mind, a poorly constructed set of financial statements could lead a decision-maker down the wrong path, by camouflaging harsh financial realities.

The type of vital feedback that will be beneficial to management include the following:

- Increased cost of goods sold resulting in decreased profitability. The income statement would reflect a reduction in "gross profit," that is, gross sales minus cost of goods sold.

- Slower customer payments resulting in tight cash flow. Signs of this condition might appear as increased "accounts receivable" on the balance sheet and reduction in cash from operations on the statement of cash flow.

- Exceedingly high vendor credit. This problem would be evidenced by higher "accounts payable" on the balance sheet and reported as a growing source of financing on the cash flow statement.

- Higher pricing coupled with cuts in expenses. Results of this strategy would be evident on the income statement where an increase in net income would be expected.

- Financial effects of a rollback in inventory purchasing. The balance sheet should highlight effects in two places, reduction in inventory and accounts payable.

- Net earnings as a percentage of total sales revenues. An income statement reflecting financial operating percentages will list these statistics.

- Loss or retirement of major items of equipment. Changes in book value of equipment would be reflected both on the balance sheet and statement of cash flow.

Surprisingly, some entrepreneurs and managers downplay the importance of financial statements. They dismiss their usefulness believing financial statements are no more than abstract information for income tax reporting or for satisfying financiers. However, by doing so they overlook numerous practical applications that could help improve the bottom line.

Answers can be found to many questions raised by management as well as external parties, especially investors and bankers. Ideally each user group should be able to read into the numbers and determine what they say about past, present and future. Consequently diminishing the role of financial statements and their applications is not an optional move for business owners.

Failing to tap into the power of financial statements would be a big mistake. By analogy a doctor who ignores obvious symptoms of disease would be regarded as inept. So too, a CEO who ignores or chooses not to take time to develop critical financial information could unnecessarily risk his or her company's financial health.

BIRD'S EYE VIEW

A closer look at the content of each report should clarify the practical uses of each financial statement. The chart below highlights the particular features of the Income Statement, Cash Flow Statement and Balance Sheet.

MANAGERIAL APPLICATIONS OF FINANCIAL STATEMENTS			
REPORT TYPE	INCOME STATEMENT	CASH FLOW STATEMENT	BALANCE SHEET
Function	Net income or loss resulting from gross revenues less expenses	Measurement of major inflows and outflows of cash	Increases and decreases in assets, liabilities and equity
Content	Specific revenue and expense line items and cumulative totals for year, quarter or month	Sources and uses of cash and cumulative totals for year, quarter or month	Categorical itemization of assets and liabilities, and balances at specified dates
Bottom Line	Net Income (Loss)	Net Increase (Decrease) in Cash	Net Increase (Decrease) in Equity

A full blown set of illustrative financial statements are provided later in this chapter. However, the chart above will serve as a quick reference on how to navigate financial statements and how to answer important questions.

With a conceptual understanding, command of terminology is the next hurdle in building proficiency in financial statement matters. Learning financial statement jargon will enable you to maximize the earning potential of your business because you will discover the true meaning behind the numbers. Functional definitions follow:

INCOME STATEMENT TERMS

Revenues comprise gross funds received in dollars or amounts owed to the company by customers from the sale of goods and services.

Expenses are the costs fully incurred by the business and typically are divided into costs of goods sold (items needed to produce a product or service) and operating expenses (items such as rent, salaries, insurance and advertising incurred in managing the business).

CASH FLOW STATEMENT TERMS

Sources of cash include net income, bank loans, and contributions by owners.

Uses of cash include loan payments, equipment purchases, and technology investments.

BALANCE SHEET TERMS

Assets include the items of value possessed by the company for future benefit. Asset value is generally equal to the lower of the purchase price or market value.

Liabilities consist of legally enforceable financial obligations such as vendor invoices, unpaid taxes and outstanding loans.

Equity is the net dollar difference between the stated values of the company assets and liabilities.

The working explanations above also illustrate the logic behind grouping dollars relating to certain activity. Even when these descriptive titles vary slightly in practice their application is the same. Regardless of business type or industry net income, cash flow and balance sheet applications are essentially the same.

GAAP Reporting

To ensure universal comparability conventional financial statements are required to adhere to certain basic accounting standards and methods. These rules are referred to as Generally Accepted Accounting Principles (GAAP). CPAs are required to observe the guidelines when preparing financial statements or when rendering a professional opinion on them.

For most non-accountants, the most important thing to remember about GAAP are their main purpose, to promote uniformity and consistency in presentation. Without commonly accepted methods of measuring gains and losses or increases and decreases in value, investors, bankers and business owners could easily be confused or misled.

Logging in all cash receipts and disbursements is only the first criteria of accounting activity regulated under GAAP. The next, and perhaps more important class of restrictive guidelines are the rules that decide how financial values are measured. . Specific criteria ranges from corporate investments, equipment, real estate and liabilities such as mortgages and long-term leases. Other rules span from write downs on items such as delinquent customer receivables to valuation of copyrights, trademarks and intellectual property.

> *The accounting rules governing presentation of income statement, balance sheet and statement of cash flows are known as generally accepted accounting principles.*

GAAP provides assurance to investors and bankers that companies are playing by the same rules. They enable third parties to compare and contrast performance under a common set of accounting standards. Entrepreneurs should also welcome these guidelines as a means for enhancing the quality of information used for decision-making.

DECISION-MAKING

Reliable financial statements are key to sound business decision-making. Consequently, it is customary for financial statements to be prepared on the basis of monthly, quarterly or annual periods. Frequent reporting is highly advisable especially for new or expanding companies.

When stacked side-by-side, year by year, varying trends in financial condition and direction are easier to spot. By examining two or more prior periods as a financial baseline the results of management strategy is more evident. For this reason in most companies, financial statement feedback is invaluable.

To improve financial performance, entrepreneurs and key decision-makers should be able to count on financial statements to quantify their financial well-being. Furthermore, lenders and investors rarely accept verbal representations of profitability, liquidity and net worth. Financial statements also serve to keep stakeholders informed and aware of a company's real financial circumstances. Financial statements are the most objective and reliable manner for determining the financial standing of a business within a particular industry.

Although entrepreneurs may direct their accountants to prepare their financial statements, they should never be out of touch with the content or quality. In the end, financial statements will be regarded as management's representations rather than those of their accountants. Quality and completeness are a reflection on management's integrity and competence. In the next chapter analytical techniques used by financiers to assess requests for funding will be reviewed in depth. For the most part these methods focus on specific segments of each of three basic financial statements.

In summary, conventional financial statements represent a well-defined system of keeping score of your financial performance and condition. Adherence to GAAP ensures the financial statements of multiple companies are comparable. While the accounting framework provides specific rules for financial reporting valuation, a reasonable amount of flexibility exists.

REAL WORLD MATTERS

Assume the CEOs of Matrix, Inc. and Potomac, LLC have arranged to meet with their respective bankers. Matrix's intention is to secure financing for expansion while Potomac has a critical need for working capital to pursue several potential large contracts. The following pages contain sample income statements, cash flow statements and balance sheets for each company. Also provided are navigation guides to help you understand statements presented.

If you were in the shoes of the banker, how would you rate their respective financial statements?

INCOME STATEMENT(S)
FOR THE YEAR ENDED DECEMBER 31, 20XX

	MATRIX, INC.	POTOMAC, LLC
REVENUES		
Maintenance Products	$10,500,000	$ --
Hospitality Products	26,000,000	--
On-Line Services		2,750,000
Software Support Services		2,250,000
Total Revenues	36,500,000	5,000,000
COST OF GOODS/SERVICES		
Cost of Goods Sold – Maintenance Products	7,350,000	$ --
Cost of Goods Sold – Hospitality Products	16,900,000	--
Direct Labor – On-Line Services		1,512,500
Direct Labor – Software Support Services		1,350,000
Total Direct Expenses	24,250,000	2,862,500
Gross Profits	12,250,000	2,137,500
DIRECT SELLING EXPENSES		
Commissions	1,830,000	--
INDIRECT EXPENSES		
Salaries and Wages (Admin & Mgmt)	2,280,000	550,000
Employer's Payroll Taxes	170,000	50,000
Equipment Leasing	480,000	140,000
Utilities	260,000	100,000
Rent – Warehouses/Office	2,500,000	260,000
Office Expenses	170,000	70,000
Insurance	140,000	50,000
Dues and Licenses	50,000	20,000
Repairs and Maintenance	80,000	40,000
Travel and Transportation	20,000	140,000
Advertising	480,000	80,000
Legal and Accounting	120,000	20,000
Interest	420,000	36,000
Depreciation	170,000	20,000
Total Expenses	9,170,000	1,576,000
Net Income Before Taxes	3,080,000	561,500
Income Tax Expense	(1,250,000)	(130,000)
NET INCOME	$1,830,000	$431,500

THE INCOME STATEMENT QUICK NAVIGATION GUIDE:	
Revenues from Sales	Under the Accrual Method of Accounting revenue is reportable at the time of billing not collection. Includes revenues from products and services, as appropriate.
Less Cost of Sales	Costs of services rendered and products actually sold. For products includes merchandise, material, assembly labor and other direct product expenses. For services includes labor, commissions and other direct service costs.
Less Operating Expenses	Under the Accrual Method expenses are recognized when incurred, not time of payment. Includes owners' and managers' salaries, office rent, insurance, advertising and other operating expenses.
Equals Net Income or Loss	Profit or loss from operations.

STATEMENT OF CASH FLOWS
FOR THE YEAR ENDED DECEMBER 31, 20XX

	MATRIX	POTOMAC
Cash Flows from Operating Activities		
Net Income from operations	$1,830,000	$431,500
Adjustments:		
Depreciation	170,000	20,000
Increase in Accounts Receivable	(100,000)	(100,000)
Increase in Merchandise Inventory	(500,000)	
Increase in Accounts Payable	250,000	(100,000)
Decrease in Sales Taxes Payable	(50,000)	
Increase in Payroll Taxes Payable	20,000	(50,000)
Net Cash Provided by Operating Activities	1,620,000	201,500
Cash Flows from Investing Activities		
Purchase of Equipment/Furnishings	(800,000)	(126,000)
Purchase of Real Estate	(200,000)	
Net Cash Used in Investing Activities	(1,000,000)	(126,000)
Cash Flows from Financing Activities		
Loans – Repayment of Principal	(520,000)	(50,500)
Net Cash Used in Financing Activities	(520,000)	(50,500)
Net Increase in Cash	100,000	25,000
Cash in Banks, Beginning of Year	320,000	60,000
Cash in Banks, End of Year	$420,000	$85,000

STATEMENT OF CASH FLOW QUICK NAVIGATION GUIDE:	
Sources of Cash	Cash inflows from all sources are identified and taken into account. **Typically they include:** • Net Cash from Operations (i.e. collections from sales less expenses paid) • Proceeds from Bank Loan • Contribution of Capital by Owners • Proceeds from Owners' Loan to Company • Other Sources of Cash
Less Uses of Cash	Outflows other than normal operating expenses are designated and reported. Typically, these items consist of the following: • Loans—Payments • Purchase of Equipment • Purchase of Real Estate • Other Cash Outflows
Equals Net Increase or Decrease in Cash	Represents the difference overall.

BALANCE SHEET
DECEMBER 31, 20XX

	MATRIX	POTOMAC
ASSETS		
Current Assets		
Cash in Banks	$420,000	$85,000
Accounts Receivable – Trade	1,500,000	240,000
Merchandise Inventory	2,420,000	--
Total Current Assets	4,320,000	325,000
Non-Current Assets		
Loans Receivable – Employees	25,000	25,000
Security Deposits	50,000	30,000
Equipment/Furnishings (Net of Accumulated Depreciation)	1,700,000	200,000
Investment in Real Estate	1,000,000	--
Total Non-Current Assets		
	2,775,000	255,000
TOTAL ASSETS	7,115,000	580,000
LIABILITIES		
Current Liabilities		
Accounts Payable – Trade	1,850,000	85,000
Sales Tax Payable	150,000	--
Payroll Taxes Payable	40,000	15,000
Loan Payable Bank – Current	420,000	50,000
Total Current Liabilities	2,460,000	150,000
Long Term Liabilities		
Loan Payable Bank – Long Term	1,780,000	250,000
Loans Payable – Officers and Shareholders	150,000	30,000
Total Long Term Liabilities		
	1,930,000	280,000
TOTAL LIABILITIES	4,390,000	430,000
EQUITY		
Common Stock/Member Capital	2,000,000	70,000
Retained Earnings/Members' Equity	725,000	80,000
Total Stockholders'/Members' Equity		
	2,725,000	150,000
TOTAL LIABILITIES AND STOCKHOLDERS'/MEMBER'S EQUITY	$7,115,000	$580,000

Checkpoints for Novices

The profiles of Matrix and Potomac display the broad range of financial data contained in a basic set of statements. If you are a novice or becoming intricately acquainted with these presentations a walk-through of the main checkpoints could be highly beneficial.

The profiles of Matrix and Potomac display the broad range of financial data contained in a basic set of statements. If you are a novice or becoming intricately acquainted with these presentations a walk-through of the main checkpoints could be highly beneficial.

The **Income Statements** for Matrix and Potomac, reveal the following:

1. Matrix's gross profit on Hospitality Products exceeds that of its Maintenance Products.

	MAINTENANCE	HOSPITALITY
Revenues	$10,500,000	$26,000,000
Cost of Goods Sold	$7,350,000	$16,900,000
Gross Profit	$3,150,000	$9,100,000

2. Potomac's On-Line Services have a higher margin than the company's Software Support Services.

	ON-LINE	SOFTWARE
Revenues	$2,750,000	$2,250,000
Cost of Goods Sold	$1,512,500	$1,350,000
Gross Profit	$1,237,500	$900,000

3. Matrix and Potomac each expended cash or financing to purchase long-term assets.

	MATRIX	POTOMAC
Net Income	$1,830,000	$431,500

The illustrative **Statements of Cash Flow** for each company pinpoint the following with respect to sources and uses of cash:

1. Matrix and Potomac each generated positive cash from their respective operations for the year.

	MATRIX	POTOMAC
Net Cash From Operations	$1,620,000	$201,500

2. For Potomac, several key operating factors minimized the amount of cash generated from operations.

Increase (build up) in Accounts Receivable	$100,000
Decrease in (pay down) of Accounts Payable to Vendors	$100,000
Decrease in (pay down) Payroll Taxes	$50,000

3. Matrix and Potomac each expended cash to purchase long term assets.

	MATRIX	POTOMAC
Purchase of Equipment/Furnishings	$800,000	$126,000
Purchase of Real Estate	200,000	0
Total Additions	$1,000,000	$126,000

4. Matrix and Potomac each used their cash to retire long term debt.

	MATRIX	POTOMAC
Repayment of Loan Principal	$520,000	$50,500

A close examination of the **Balance Sheet** of each company will shows the following:

1. Total assets reported by Matrix and Potomac respectively:

	MATRIX	POTOMAC
Total Assets	$7,115,000	$580,000

2. The most liquid assets of each company can be found classified under "Current Assets."

	MATRIX	POTOMAC
Cash In Banks	$420,000	$ 85,000
Accounts Receivable	1,500,000	240,000
Merchandise Inventory	2,420,000	0
Total Current Assets	$4,340,000	$325,000

3. Total liabilities having a maturity (payment due date) of one year or less are classified under the heading of "Current Liabilities".

	MATRIX	POTOMAC
Total Current Liabilities	$2,460,000	$150,000

4. Total amount of equity (net worth) of each company is presented under the heading "Equity:"

	MATRIX	POTOMAC
Total Stockholders'/ Members' Equity	$2,725,000	$150,000

NOTABLE REFLECTIONS AT A GLANCE

✦ Conventional financial statements consist of the Income Statement, Cash Flow Statement and Balance Sheet.

✦ Conventional financial statements document financial activity holistically.

✦ Regular financial statement review and analysis serves to improve overall financial performance.

✦ Reliable and accurate financial statements are essential for strategic planning and business valuation.

✦ Investors and bankers rely on financial statements, not words.

✦ An ability to interpret financial statements is key to managing growth, costs, and profitability.

CHAPTER SIX
Monitor Vital Signs...
Build Economic Stamina

| *The Journey* |

BJ and Taylor continue to meet regularly to reflect on their respective business aspirations, challenges and opportunities. Even though Matrix has been relatively successful financially, the company has areas of weakness that have become quite visible under close scrutiny.

After completing several financial ratio computations the company's banker suggested Matrix appeared to be losing steam. The banker noticed that Matrix's inventory turnover ratio was decreasing; indicating inventory may not be moving off the shelves as quickly as it did in the past. Likewise, the average days' sales in accounts receivable had climbed upward suggesting customer collections have slowed in proportion to sales revenue.

BJ invited Taylor to chime in on the banker's comment, and the friends discussed possible reasons for the fall off. They wondered whether Matrix' was unknowingly overstocking certain goods no longer in high demand. The idea also surfaced that Matrix's customer credit screening may need to be revamped to ensure credit is being granted selectively.

BJ intends to expand the financial analysis into other operating and financial activities. For instance, he would like to review fluctuations in ratios and percentages applicable to his cash flow, debt coverage and return on investment. Even though Matrix obtained additional funding a year ago, he wants to better understand why profitability had not increased as much as anticipated. In addition, he would like to verify that Matrix is still in compliance with each of the financial covenants of its bank loan. The contract provisions stipulate that certain minimum financial thresholds must be maintained especially in the area of debt coverage.

You are frantic! You just learned that your company's current debt level may to have exceeded the maximum allowable limit established under its bank loan agreement. This shocking discovery occurred just as you were about to forward your most recent financial statements to your banker in advance of making a request for additional financing.

While investigating the underlying cause for the jump in debt, you also realize cash in the bank is much lower than normal. In fact, recent bank statements reveal unexplained electronic transfers and automatic debits to the account. Other than withdrawals covering your regular monthly bank loan payment, you do not recall authorizing any other automatic bank debits or electronic transfers.

Even if you have never specifically experienced either of the dilemmas described above you no doubt can imagine how easy it might be to get into debt over your head or be the victim of financial impropriety without a built in alarm system. To avoid possible disaster, seasoned veterans agree it is much better to prevent rather than cure these problems.

Financial monitoring and oversight should be an everyday function. With this in mind, a host of safeguards designed to improve your ability to monitor and protect business assets in an efficient but highly-effective manner will be examined in depth in this chapter. Along with these tools, the type of financial control measures financiers most favor will be highlighted.

CHAPTER HIGHLIGHTS:

→ Measuring Health and Wellness

→ Key Percentages and Ratios

→ Industry Norms

→ Financial Safeguards

→ Second Opinions

HEALTH AND WELLNESS

You may ask what constitutes sound financial health and wellness. The simple answer lies with at least a dozen different quantifiable and qualitative factors. These readings are mostly tied to profitability, efficiency, and liquidity. However without a basic overview, the average business person may not fully understand how these parameters should be interpreted.

For instance, rarely will a banker or financier rely exclusively on financial statements to judge the health and wellness of a company. Financial statements prepared according to Generally Accepted Accounting Principles (GAAP) are intended to be informative for a general audience. Accordingly, financiers as a whole will demand far more detailed feedback and disclosure. Depending on the amount of funding involved financiers will insist on a complete financial DNA.

Issues that most often raise concerns relate to financial stability and profitability. For example, where a company has experienced a high sales growth rate but simultaneously a decline in net earnings. A sudden build up in the balance of accounts receivables at a much faster rate than new sales growth will likewise raise eyebrows. Also, when maturing debts skyrocket while sales remain flat, most observers will conclude financial trouble is imminent. A savvy person possessing analytical skill will be able to spot these adverse conditions with a simple review of financial vital signs.

In top tier financing circles it is customary to perform a complete financial inspection of an investee company up front. Investors and bankers commonly refer to this as "due diligence." The process spills over into various financial, operational as well as legal affairs of a company. Knowledge and understanding of conventional practices can be a major advantage when making a pitch for funding.

> *Knowledge and understanding of conventional due diligence procedures can be a major advantage when making a pitch for funding.*

THE DIAGNOSTIC PROCESS

Financiers routinely request independent verification of bank account balances, make various inquiries with professional advisors as well as require assurances from CPAs about the quality of company financial statements. Files and records covering major customer and supplier relationships, existing bank and equipment loans can also be the focus of attention.

Usually when a large amount of funding is involved no stone will be left unturned. Even the credit standing of the principal owners of a business could be scrutinized especially if their personal guarantees are pledged to collateralize financing. For that matter, depending on the need for collateral pledges of inventory, equipment, and machinery may be required. Lastly, documents relating to valuable property rights such as licenses, leases and royalties will be scrutinized.

Just as entrepreneurs, CEOs and managers regularly devote significant time to operational matters of importance, they also regularly assess their company's financial strengths and weaknesses from the perspective of an outsider. The objective is not only to identify areas that will raise concerns about financial stability and profitability but to devise a plan to remedy underlying defects.

The scope of a thorough health evaluation of course will depend on the nature of the business. For instance, assessing a dry cleaner will normally take far less analysis than an engineering or manufacturing firm.

At the early stage, it is important to understand that financiers initially distinguish high and low investment opportunities largely based on a combination of the rules of thumb cited below:

- A debt-to-worth ratio that exceeds 4-to-1 may be a sign of too heavy debt load.
- Accounts payable in excess of cash in banks, accounts receivable and inventory may indicate higher risk of insolvency.
- Inventory stock sixty days over pending customer orders may be a sign of declining marketability of merchandise inventory.

- Increased overall labor costs after a period of flat or declining sales may be indicative of poor financial management controls.

- Persistent bank overdrafts may be a sign of an undercapitalized business.

- Loan to value (LTV) of assets in excess of 70% to 80 % may indicate that equity capital is more suitable than debt funding.

After these basic observations a more in depth assessment is usually conducted. Understandably, investors and bankers want to rule out any insurmountable health problems.

NORMS AND BENCHMARKS

A very reliable indication of the financial state of a business, is how well it scores in relation to operating norms and standards within its own industry. Industry specific vital signs are considered highly indicative of a strong or weak performing company.

In the context of norms and benchmarks, a business is expected to demonstrate their worth when stacked against their peers. Sometimes the test is tough to pass because frontrunners enjoy a capital and operating advantage that allows them to function more cost effectively. Nevertheless, up and comers should be able to register high marks for versatility, efficiency and return on investment.

Peer data including industry and trade association information is almost universally relied on to grade a company's strategies and tactics. Pertinent data is ordinarily segmented based on dollar ranges of assets and revenues. Staying current and knowledgeable of the financial norms and standards within the applicable ranges is advisable. All things being equal, you do not want to allow your business to fall too far behind the pack.

A sample illustration of average financial operating percentages for medium size companies in the U.S. printing, computer services and construction industries is shown in the chart on the following page.

Industry performance data displayed above is indicative of the type of data base used by financiers and others to gauge financial performance for companies they consider investing in. When stacked next to the income statement of companies in these particular industries both positive and negative qualities are more detectable. For example, if your computer system and design services company's net income to sales percentage is significantly less than the six percent as listed in the chart, this may be indicative of operating weakness. At a minimum, both a financier and business owner would be interested in investigating the circumstances. In this sense, peer norms help to facilitate constructive discussion.

However, just because a company is out of step with industry norms does not necessarily mean it is underperforming. There may be valid and compelling business reasons for deviation. For example, a decision to rent more warehouse space in anticipation of a future contract could impose a higher than average rent expense. Similarly, it may be incumbent to pay higher wage rates based on

A comparative industry review of financial performance should include analysis and investigation of substantial differences.

competitive pay ranges within a certain geographic region. Generally speaking, these type of explanations rule out what might otherwise be a negative finding.

Routine reviews and comparisons of industry information also offers a roadmap for improving financial returns. A bird's eye view of

Comparative Financial Norms
Net Income and Operating Expenses/Average Percent of Revenues

Industry	Computer & System Design Services (Assets $1million - $5 million)	Newspaper Printing & Publishing (Assets $1million - $5million)	General Contractors & Heavy Construction (Assets $250,000 - $1 million)
Revenue	100.00%	100.00%	100.00%
Cost of Goods Sold	43.90%	31.70%	75.20%
Officer Compensation	5.20%	8.80%	4.00%
Other Salaries & Wages	22.00%	20.60%	3.80%
Employee Benefits	1.20%	1.00%	0.60%
Pension & Profit Sharing	0.70%	0.60%	0.30%
Rent	1.50%	0.80%	0.80%
Taxes (exc. federal income)	3.20%	3.30%	1.90%
Depreciation	0.90%	5.10%	1.70%
Interest Expense	0.40%	2.20%	0.70%
Advertising	0.50%	1.00%	0.30%
Repairs	n/a	1.30%	0.60%
Other Expenses	14.50%	16.50%	5.70%
Total Expenses	93.30%	92.90%	95.60%
Net Income	6.10%	7.10%	4.40%

the business and financial performance of others could lead to formulating new strategies or revising old ones. Tracking industry specific trends is also an effective means for staying abreast of nuances in your industry.

GENERIC VITAL SIGNS

It is helpful to think of financial measures in terms of a MRI. Generally, they are designed to help detect and assess laden conditions. By analogy, in assessing a person's health, imaging feedback is sometimes used to spot abnormalities. Similarly in business, various financial markers are routinely relied upon to determine which, if any, of the important financial working parts are out of alignment.

There are at least a dozen financial measures of a generic nature that are considered crucial to check on a regular basis. These indicators mainly focus on liquidity, cash flow, asset turnover, debt capacity, earnings and operating efficiency. Each metric is linked to at least one of the three basic financial statements, namely, the balance sheet, income statement and statement of cash flow.

It is wise for every key decision maker to have a basic understanding and knowledge of these generic vital signs. A proper application and interpretation is key for any business bent on attracting financing. Much like basic financial statements, these metrics belong in every entrepreneur's management handbook.

For ease of interpretation these so called generic vital signs are described and illustrated below based on the sample financial statements in chapter five.

RATIO NAMES	EXPLANATIONS AND USES	RATIO FORMULAS	MATRIX *
Accounts Receivables:			
Accounts Receivable Ratio:	Turning over accounts receivable rapidly builds working capital and nurtures a positive cash flow. A turnover ratio measures the length of time required to record and collect payment on credit sales.	Net Credit Sales ÷ Average A/R	24 turns
Average Days Sales in Accounts Receivables	This ratio measures how many days worth of sales are tied up in accounts receivables and indicates how efficiently you are collecting from customers.	365 Days ÷ Accounts Receivable Turnover Ratio	15 days
Inventory Management:			
Turnover Ratio	The average length of time it takes to turn merchandise into customer sales affects working capital. Turnover ratio measures the number of times inventory is turned over during a specified period.	Cost of Goods Sold ÷ Average Inventory	10 turns
Cash Flow Management:			
Long-Term Debt	This ratio measures the sufficiency of cash flow from operations to cover debt payment obligations.	Long-Term Debt Payments ÷ Cash From Operations	0.13
Debt Coverage	This ratio measures the sufficiency of cash flow from operations to cover total debt.	Total Debt ÷ Cash From Operations	0.72
Cash Flow to Sales	This ratio measures the efficiency with which sales result in cash flow.	Cash From Operations ÷ Sales	0.09
Operational Index	This ratio measures the relationship between cash flow generated during a period and net income during the same period.	Cash From Operations ÷ Net Income	1.78
* Reference financial statements in Chapter 5			

Cash Flow to Debt	Many analysts feel that this ratio is the best single indicator of a firm's solvency. A rough view of cash flow is net income plus depreciation.	(New Income + Depreciation) ÷ Total Debt	1.39
Interest Coverage:			
Times Interest Earned	The Times Interest Earned ratio is a valuable tool in analyzing leverage financing. It provides for the relationship between earnings and interest charges. This ratio measures the number of times that interest cost is earned by a company as a result of its operations. The higher the ratio the stronger the coverage. A minimum ratio is 1 to 1; a typical guideline is from 3 to 1.	Earnings Before Interest and Taxes ÷ Total Interest	20.59
Total Interest coverage	This ratio analyzes the firm's ability to repay interest and make the principal periodic repayments. This ratio clearly indicates to the banker the firm's cash flow available for debt service.	(Earnings Before Interest and Taxes) ÷ (Total Interest + Principal Payments)	5.93
Rates of Return:			
Return on Equity	Measures how effectively owner and investor funds are leveraged to generate income.	Net Income (during a period of time) ÷ Net Worth (at beginning of period)	
Return on Assets	Measures how effectively a company leverages all its assets (both current and long-term) to generate income.	Net Income (during a period of time) ÷ Total Assets (at beginning of period)	

Financial ratios are analogous to player stats. In baseball, hitters evaluate their batting average, pitchers the number of earned runs allowed, and base runners their steals versus the number of attempts.

In professional football quarterbacks study their passing attempts and completions; running backs their carries and average yards; and receivers their receptions and yards gained after the catch. Just as these statistics help athletes to evaluate and improve their performance, a regular review of your company's financial vital signs holds this potential benefit as well.

FINANCIAL SAFEGUARDS

In general, safeguards over the finances of a business are commonly known as internal controls. They are designed to help minimize risk for undetected accounting errors, fraud and other financial irregularities. Because many small but growing businesses lean heavy on a few people to administer the accounting functions of the business, adequate safeguards are crucial. Indeed, even many large companies fall victim to crippling errors and fraud when their system of checks and balances falls apart.

At the outset of this chapter I raised a hypothetical scenario involving a business owner who discovered unexplained electronic transfers appearing on their company bank statements. In real life this could prove to be a valid transaction but one that he or she was simply uninformed about. On the other hand, there is always a possibility under these circumstances that an odd looking item is just the tip of the iceberg.

In the midst of developing a business and dealing with a litany of demands, business owners are less inclined to pay adequate attention to financial safeguards. In fact, most fraud occurs because financial related duties and responsibilities are concentrated in the hands of a single individual, while the owner is pre-occupied. Ideally, to promote cross-checking financial related duties and responsibilities should be divided among several different people.

Separation of duties guards against the possibility that someone in the processing chain will make an intentional or unintentional error without notice. Needless to say no company can thrive monetarily when financial errors, improprieties or misdeeds are permitted without repercussion. History is replete with both small and large businesses that collapsed after being sidelined by financial indiscretions that probably could have been deterred.

Legislation makes internal control review and improvement a requirement for publicly owned companies. The Sarbanes-Oxley Act enacted into law in 2002 regulates issues such as corporate governance and financial reporting, and it penalizes public companies for inaccurate or incomplete financial disclosure.

Sarbanes-Oxley also stipulates public companies must subject themselves to a comprehensive review of their internal controls no more than 90 days before releasing material financial information relating to the company and its consolidated subsidiaries. This legislation epitomizes the cliché, "trust but verify."

Nowadays, internal control examinations are considered best practices for public companies. Adopting this practice as a means of quality assurance also could prove beneficial for entrepreneurial companies as well. Financial security should be considered paramount to protecting assets of a business with the main objective being to:

- Safeguard assets from misuse or misappropriation.

- Verify that business resources were utilized for business purposes only.

- Maintain reliable record keeping systems that promote financial reporting accuracy.

- Promote compliance with control policies and procedures.

As earlier suggested small businesses often struggle to accomplish these objectives with only a few staff persons. In some cases, the owner may have to continually be the source of direct authorization, approval and review of certain financial translations. In any environment, the following general guidelines could be helpful in strengthening a basic system of internal controls:

CUSTOMER REMITTANCES

- Consider bonding employees who handle substantial amounts of cash.

- Route incoming customer remittances to someone other than the person responsible for maintaining the accounting system and posting bank deposits.

- Customer remittances received should be stamped "for deposit only."

- Bank deposits should be made on a daily basis and funds secured until deposited.

- Over-the-counter cash collections should be tracked and accounted for at the end of each shift.

DISBURSEMENT OF FUNDS

- Persons with bank signature should not have access to restricted accounting duties and responsibilities.

- Bank statements should be reviewed and reconciled monthly by someone not responsible for making deposits or processing checks.

- Accounting related documents such as customer invoices and bank checks should be pre-numbered to assure accountability.

- Bank signatory authority should be highly restricted.

- Access to accounting software and other systems should be highly restricted.

- Payments should be approved only with an invoice or other documentation.

PETTY CASH OVERSIGHT

- Custody of petty cash should be limited.

- Supporting voucher requests should be used to authorize disbursements.

- The fund should be counted and reconciled on a regular basis by someone other than the custodian.

- A dollar balance ceiling should be established.

- A reconciliation of supporting vouchers, invoices and other documentation should be performed regularly by someone other than the custodian.

RECEIVABLES ADMINISTRATION

- Customer purchase orders, billing statements and shipping documents should be maintained.

- A reconciliation of activity based on the documents noted should be performed.

PAYROLL PROCESSING

- Employee hires and terminations should be verified independently.

- Access to payroll processing systems and records should be highly restricted.

- Payroll should not be processed by those responsible for processing hires and terminations.

ACCOUNTING FOR INVENTORY EQUIPMENT

- Physical inventories should be taken on a regular basis.

- High dollar items should be tracked and accounted for by serial number.

- Physical counts and values should be reconciled to accounting records.

SECOND OPINIONS

In most cases an assurance regarding your company's financial statements from an outside third party can be extremely beneficial. An outside perspective serves as another type of internal control regarding the accounting and financial reporting process. Additionally, whether you employ one person or a department to handle accounting functions an outsider will provide, at a minimum, another level of review.

There is growing pressure on companies of all sizes to become more accountable for generating high quality and reliable financial statements. More businesses are engaging CPAs to provide a written assurance about the fair presentation of their financial statements. The professional opinion of a CPA adds credibility to the numbers and thereby comfort to outside stakeholders.

The CPA's written opinion principally speaks to a company's adherence to GAAP. In this regard, CPAs provide three types of assurance services. From lowest to highest these assurances are labeled compilation, review and audit. In each case, the CPA provides a written report that accompanies the financial statements and reporting. A snapshot of these underlying processes is provided on the following page.

A compilation is the representation of management (the owners) and is limited to presenting in the form of financial statements. CPAs do not audit or review the financial statements and, accordingly, do not express an opinion or any other form of assurance on them.

A review consists principally of inquiries of company personnel and analytical procedures applied to financial data. It is substantially less in scope than an audit in accordance with generally accepted auditing standards, the objective of which is the expression of an opinion regarding the financial statements taken as a whole. Accordingly, CPAs do not express such as opinion.

An audit includes examining, on a test basis, evidence supporting the amounts and disclosures in the financial statements. An audit also includes assessing the accounting principles used for significant estimates made by management, as well as evaluating the overall financial statement presentation. Audits provide a reasonable basis for CPAs opinion on whether the financial statements are presented fairly in all material respects.

To the Board of Directors
Matrix, Inc.
Baltimore, Maryland

INDEPENDENT AUDITOR'S REPORT

We have audited the accompanying balance sheets of Matrix, Inc. as of
December 31, 20XX and 20XX, and the related statements of income,
retained earnings, and cash flows for the years then ended. These financial
statements are the responsibility of the company's management. Our
responsibility is to express an opinion on these financial statements based on
our audits.

We conducted our audits in accordance with auditing standards generally
accepted in the United States of America. Those standards require that we
plan and perform the audit to obtain reasonable assurance about whether
the financial statements are free of material misstatement. An audit includes
examining, on a test basis, evidence supporting the amounts and disclosures
in the financial statements. An audit also includes assessing the accounting
principles used and significant estimates made by management, as well as
evaluating the overall financial statement presentation. We believe that our
audits provide a reasonable basis for our opinion.

In our opinion, the financial statements referred to above present fairly, in
all material respects, the financial position of Matrix, Inc. as of December
31, 20XX and 20XX, and the results of its operations and its cash flows
for the years then ended in conformity with accounting principles generally
accepted in the United States of America.

Bennett, Hutt & Co., L.L.C.
Columbia, Maryland
February 15, 20XX

To best appreciate the end result of an audit, a sample of a standard unqualified opinion is presented on the previous page.

For any company anticipating a public or private stock offering in the near future a financial statement audit is highly recommended. Audited financial statements are usually required by regulators who oversee private and public offerings. On the other hand, a "review" or "compilation" may be acceptable for privately-owned businesses which take on no more than bank financing.

From a cost perspective, compilations and reviews are generally less expensive than audits because the CPA's scope of work is not nearly as extensive. Neither one entails an in-depth inspection, testing, and analytical work called for in an audit. At a bare minimum, compilations are generally advised for small businesses with no major outside financing.

NOTABLE REFLECTIONS AT A GLANCE

→ Financial health measurements comprise conventional financial percentages and ratios.

→ Critical vital signs include financial liquidity, profitability, cash flow, asset turnover and debt capacity.

→ Performance comparisons allow businesses to be ranked and evaluated.

→ Rules of thumb determine financial wellness based on debt to equity, accounts receivable turnover and other financial relationships.

→ Assurances from CPAs in the form of compilation, review and audit add credibility to financial statements.

→ Financial checks and balances safeguard assets and deter misuse.

CHAPTER SEVEN
Accelerate the Breakthrough ...
Finance the Dream

| *The Journey* |

In the past, Matrix relied solely on debt financing to raise capital because BJ had reservations about sharing ownership and control. He now realizes his company may have grown faster and more profitability had he been more flexible in his thinking.

Taylor Made—having experienced a leveling off in sales growth—believes equity funding could provide the resources necessary for her to pursue emerging business opportunities with less worry about short-term cash flow. She is committed to fully evaluating the pros and cons of venture capital versus debt financing. BJ hopes to explore different debt financing alternatives. However, both are willing to consider a combination of debt and equity financing. However, because of Taylor's lack of familiarity, she is extremely apprehensive about financing.

"Finance your business with other people's money" is a widely used cliché that is quite misleading. It suggests financing a business is simply a matter of advertising for investors without any need to look to make a sizable investment of your own. Nothing could be further from the truth.

Financing a business with other people's money requires success in jumping through certain hoops as well as an ability to deliver a return on investment. Rarely, will raising capital be a simple proposition. There are multiple steps and hurdles that must be overcome.

Similar to an entrepreneur's intent to increase earnings, financiers aim to maximize return on their investment. Furthermore, private investors, banks and other lending institutions strive to profit at the lowest possible risk. In essence entrepreneurs and financiers share the same financial objective. Accordingly, forging an alliance means carving out a win-win for both parties.

Securing capital requires strategic planning and attention to detail. In order to gain confidence and interest, an entrepreneur and CEO must have a credible business plan that clearly outlines financing needs and requirements. At a minimum, when seeking debt, projected cash generated from operations should be sufficient to service debt payments. On the other hand, where there is only pure investment capital, the prospect for a return on investment has to more than justify the risk.

Aside from meeting the economic thresholds for debt or equity, companies seeking financing must also have the capacity to comply with all necessary financial reporting requirements. For purposes of monitoring their investment, both lenders and investors will insist on reliable financial statements.

In terms of documentation, financing deals typically encompass a litany of contractual terms and obligations that should be carefully and thoughtfully considered. In their excitement and zeal to obtain funding, entrepreneurs sometimes only gloss over terms and conditions which later prove to be unduly one-sided, cost prohibitive or overly restrictive.

The small print in financing agreements can sour the terms of the deal. Consequently, hasty decisions should always be avoided. Hurried transactions may be alluring at first look, but under scrutiny, overly restrictive and far too expensive. Provisions relating to maximum funding limits, repayment period, minimum or guaranteed payments, collateral demands, and early pay-off also have to be evaluated very closely. Make no mistake—when it comes to financing—there are no free lunches.

Shopping for financing should not start until the entrepreneur has a clear understanding of financing alternatives, informational requirements, pricing approaches and the underwriting standards.

CHAPTER HIGHLIGHTS:

→ Common Types of Business Financing

→ Understanding and Quantifying Financing Needs

→ Criteria for Selecting a Financial Partner

→ Shopping Your Deal

→ Preparing a Successful Financing Request

THE FAST TRACK

The major barrier to growth is access to capital. Without adequate capital, even the most promising business will languish between making just enough to pay the bills and not enough to take the company one step higher. Proven strategies for raising capital are precious.

A company world renowned for traveling the fast track to secure capital to finance growth is Google.

> Google was founded in 1996 by two Stanford University graduate students, Larry Page and Sergey Brin. Unable to afford new computers, the pair worked on borrowed University equipment, funded expenses on credit cards, and located their first data center in Larry's dorm room. Initially the pair sought to license their technology to an outside party.
>
> When existing companies rejected the partners' licensing offer, Larry and Sergey decided to further develop the technology in their own firm. They needed cash to set up a commercial space and repay their credit cards. A friend of a faculty member believed the company had a great deal of potential and invested $100,000 in Google. Ultimately the company raised $1 million in its first round of equity financing.
>
> By early 1999 Google had moved twice, first to a garage and then to an office building. It was answering more than 500,000 queries a day and had been named one of the world's Top 100 Web Sites by PC magazine. Additional funding was needed to keep Google expanding.
>
> In June 1999 Google secured $25 million in funding from two venture capital firms. Each firm took a seat on the Google board of directors and the board became populated with individuals who had helped grow Sun Mircrosystems,

Intuit, Amazon and Yahoo!. Key employees were hired and the firm continued to expand.

Google continued to mature by improving its technology, entering into partnerships with other internet service providers and adding products such as Google News, AdWords and Google Compute. Its growth has been explosive.

In 2004, Google's owners decided to take the company public. The initial public offering ("IPO") raised roughly $1.7 billion, making it the largest internet IPO of its time and one of the largest IPOs in history. The IPO provided cash for expansion and enabled early investors to cash out.[1]

In the span of just six years, Goggle progressed from a mom and pop operation to a publicly traded corporation valued at roughly $23 billion. Clearly, the company's ascent would not have materialized without sufficient capital financing.

Perhaps the most notable thing about the Goggle story is the evolving financing strategies. As highlighted in the synopsis, the company utilized different financing methods and toggled between various financing sources. Although your particular strategy may differ, Google provides basic lessons to take away. A search for alternative financing may be prompted by the opportunity to lower interest rates or to secure a higher credit limit. On the other hand, friends and family may be the best source of funding for start-up businesses. Strategically refinancing debt may serve to free up cash flow. Regardless of your motivation, the financing approaches discussed in this chapter should be helpful.

Financing Business Development

The very discussion of financing ordinarily triggers a plethora of reaction among business people, both positive and negative. While readily citing many trials and tribulations most business people will readily agree that gaining access to capital is key to success.

The process itself teaches entrepreneurs and CEOs learn many valuable lessons. For example, a common discovery is how challenging it is for a newly-formed business to attract capital. Most banks frown on start-ups that lack a past track record of earnings. By and large commercial financing institutions such as banks are risk adverse compared to the private and public investor community.

Whether you operate a new or mature business, financing has many dos and don'ts just pertaining to the amount of requested funding. Many wonder should the request equal or exceed what is really needed, whether it is wise to search for capital before or after the need actually arises, and whether debt or equity capital is preferable or necessary. These questions are among the key issues that will be addressed in the following pages.

The rudiments of financing are the same regardless of business or industry. At the outset, financing for start-up companies begins with the owners tapping their personal savings in order to launch their businesses. For the fortunate, their families and friends are willing to chip in financial support at an early stage. On the other hand, as a business picks up steam they will inevitably turn to outside financing to finance growth and expansion.

A build up in accounts receivable is the most common impetus for seeking bank financing. Rarely is it feasible for a business to extend customer credit without leaking cash flow. Most of the time, customer remittances arrive too late to provide the cash needed to pay creditors by the payment due date. Without some type of gap financing, this timing differential will burn up cash reserves.

Financing expansion is somewhat like funding the purchase of a residence; few people have the means to purchase a home outright without a mortgage. Similarly, few entrepreneurs have the means to finance growth out of pocket.

Business growth and development usually spur a need for long and intermediate financing. Sales growth puts pressure on cash reserves. Increasing demand escalates production costs and begs for enhanced infrastructure. Essentially, businesses find it necessary to increase space and acquire equipment. Fast growing entrepreneurial companies like Google are forced to mature early. They quickly have to weigh their financing options: equity, debt, or most commonly some combination thereof.

For most companies it is not possible to convert sales into cash fast enough to meet internal demand, outside financing is crucial.

Funds provided to a business at a specific rate of interest with a definite and immediate repayment schedule constitutes "debt." The interest rate may be fixed or variable, and repayment may be in installments or in full. Collateral typically is required to support debt repayment.

Money contributed to a business with a more flexible repayment schedule and less certain repayment timetable generally is referred to as "equity." Repayment of investment normally comes from profits, sale of the company's assets, merger with another company or a significant refinancing. Because of its inherent risks, equity investors typically assume more active control and participation in business affairs.

THE EQUITY OPTION

Generally speaking, equity offers a more flexible repayment structure than debt. Equity has a far less certain prospect of repayment. Equity is thought of as "patient money," because timing distributions to investors typically are tied to future earnings. In the absence of earnings, investors are left to sit and wait for return of their money. For this very reason, equity investors are less fixated on historical financial results and more focused on forecasted financial performance.

Dividends are the distribution of earnings to owners (shareholders) of a corporation. In most states payment of dividends is discretionary by law. A majority of the board of directors of a company must vote in favor of a payout after considering current profits, accumulated earning and future needs of the business. Similarly, in a limited liability company, earnings left over are technically available for distribution to owners (members).

Equity funding usually is the method of choice for raising a relatively large amount of capital.

Selling ownership or equity is a mainstay for raising relatively large sums of investment dollars. Capital intensive businesses known to frequently tap capital markets include real estate, manufacturing, technology and research and development, just to name a few.

Many businesses that became icons overnight have been launched with equity capital. Owners raised millions of dollars selling stock in the public market and utilized the funds productively to generate enormous financial gain. "Going public" means selling equity interests in the company to the general public, typically with the assistance of an investment banker. Because only a small percentage of all companies meet the stringent requirements for going public only a relative few choose this route.

Venture funds are a special subset of equity financing most germane to entrepreneurial businesses. Unlike public equity, venture capitalists seek investment opportunities with early stage and start-up companies, where risk of failure is higher, but the potential for significant financial returns is strongest. These funding sources are well-suited for a company with a marginal financial history but solid prospects for future growth and earnings. Moreover, venture capitalists place great emphasis on growth potential and less, to some extent, on past performance.

Venture capitalists bet on the upside potential of companies. Only a small percent of firms submitting proposals to venture funds receive the investments they seek.

Venture capital typically is made available through the auspices of a venture fund created on behalf of pension funds, institutional investors, and high net worth individuals. Generally, venture funds invest $1 million or more in companies growing at a rate of 50% or more each year. A sub-class of these investors—financiers who provide private equity on a smaller scale—are known as "angel investors." Angel investors often will consider smaller deals (those under $1 million) as well as larger ones as funds allow.

As suggested, high performance expectations accompany venture capital financing. Most venture capital funds aim to double, triple or possibly quadruple their money within five to seven years. To further enhance the prospects for success, these investors typically seek active participation in management and may insist on a seat on the company's board of directors.

Given the high level of financial risk assumed by venture capital investors it is no surprise these deals often involve a legal option allowing the investor to exit or acquire additional shares of ownership after a specified period. These options are couched in the form of "puts" and "calls." Through a put the investor reserves the legal right to force the owner to purchase its shares at a predetermined price if the company fails to significantly increase the value of the company, sell the company's assets or go public. On the other hand, investors may consent to a call provision that permits the company to force the investor to return its shares at a predetermined price if the company exceeds its growth and earnings targets.

Because venture capital funds are highly selective in making investments only a very small percentage of entrepreneurs who submit proposals to venture funds receive a favorable response, the majority of entrepreneurial companies pursue investments from family and friends or conventional debt financing.

THE DEBT ROUTE

In contrast to equity, debt capital fixes certain repayment obligations. The trappings of a loan business normally include a principal loan amount, an interest rate and a repayment term measured in months or years. By its very nature, debt requires amortization, that is, regular payment of principal and interest until the outstanding balance is repaid in full.

The standard operating procedure of conventional lenders is straight forward: secure repayment of the principal loan amount; collect agreed upon interest on the amount of funds advanced; and in the event of default, take possession of assets pledged as collateral and if necessary pursue assets of personal and corporate guarantors. Even with worthy collateral, most lenders will not approve a loan unless the risk of default is relatively low. Commercial lenders prefer a borrower with the ability to generate more than enough earnings to service the loan.

Lenders' objectives are fairly simple: secure repayment of the principal loan amount; collect agreed upon interest on the amount of funds advanced; and in the event of default, take possession of assets pledged as collateral.

Purveyors of debt capital work to safeguard their investments by requiring the borrower to demonstrate an ability to repay the loan from earnings. In addition, a pledge of collateral is stipulated in case the loan cannot be repaid. Sources of collateral may include real estate, equipment, inventory, accounts receivable and marketable securities.

When there is a deficiency in repayment, lenders commonly invoke collateral rights or a personal guarantee supplied from owners.

In some communities, publicly sponsored economic development agencies supply loan guarantees to eligible businesses. A private or public guarantee obligates the issuing party (the guarantor) to repay the loan in the event of default by the primary borrower. This additional source of repayment may make lenders more comfortable and enable them to fund projects that otherwise would not be bankable.

Prior to approving a loan, banks scrutinize company cash flows, earning projections and financial statements with great intensity. Like equity investors, even after making a loan, commercial lenders actively monitor the financial performance of their borrowers. At a minimum, they require borrowers to submit financial statements and other performance reports annually, quarterly, and sometimes even weekly or monthly. These reporting requirements allow lenders to track borrowers' financial performance and resources.

The loan evaluation and negotiation process may be quite extensive and sometimes exhaustive. Unlike venture capital funds commercial lenders have to exert their influence and control at the outset because they usually have little interaction with borrowers after the loan has been funded.

MENU A LA CARTE

When the need for financing arises, the proverbial question is, "Which type of financing makes the most sense?" In reviewing choices and alternatives the following simple ground rules are worth noting:

Short-term financing should only be used where money is needed for a period of one year or less; intermediate term, for one to five years; and long-term, for more than five years. Based on these guidelines an appropriate repayment period parallels the life span of the underlying asset being financed or, in case of working capital, a time period that corresponds with projected future earnings.

By way of illustration, if a business intends to borrow funds to purchase vehicles, the minimum financing term should be at least three and possibly five years. The equipment involved has a beneficial life cycle of several years or more, therefore the appropriate term of financing should be in the intermediate range. On the other hand, if the purpose of the funding is to liquefy accounts receivable, the funding mechanism should be short term and tailored to accommodate normal turnover of between 30 to 60 days – up to 90 days if a significant portion of the customer base consists of government agencies.

To avoid the various tiers of financing from becoming misaligned entrepreneurs should review their funding portfolios on a regular basis. Common debt financing alternatives are summarized below.

Working Capital Line of Credit	A line of credit is one of the most common financing vehicles available to small companies. The LOC consists of a specific sum made available by a bank to a qualifying company to draw on as needed over a prescribed period, usually one year. Typically the borrower is required to repay the line periodically, then the firm may reuse the funds.
Accounts Receivable Financing	Accounts receivable financing is a loan that uses accounts receivable as the primary source of repayment. The lender usually advances 70% to 80% of the adjusted accounts receivable balance. The business can repay and re-borrow any amount up to the agreed upon percentage of its adjusted accounts receivable balance.

Factoring	Factoring is a purchase of accounts receivable as they arise. The business submits orders as they are received to the factor for approval. In turn the factor advances the funds (less a discount for bad accounts and a financing charge) to the business. Receivables are paid directly to the factorer.
Term Financing	Term loans are available in a variety of forms and are structured according to the length of use of the item(s) for which the proceeds will be applied. They also reflect repayment conditions consistent with availability of the primary sources of repayment. Most often obtained for equipment purchases such as computers, vehicles, furniture and machinery.
Asset Based Borrowing	Most simplistically asset based lending refers to any loan secured by an asset. Mortgages and receivables factoring are asset based loans. Usually, however, asset based lending is used to describe loans secured by assets not normally used to secure loans. Intellectual property and trademarks may be collateral for asset based loans. Typically, these loans are riskier and more expensive than other types of financing.
Mortgage Borrowing	Mortgage loans are generally long-term loans with maturities of 15 years or more secured by real property.

"BREAD AND BUTTER" ISSUES

A strong case for financing answers three key questions: "Why your company needs financing?" "How much funding is required?" and "How and when the funds will be repaid?" A company that is prepared to offer unequivocal answers to these questions has a much stronger chance of obtaining funding.

BASIC FINANCING NEEDS

When company executives initially decide additional financing will be necessary to progress the factors driving the need it may not always be obvious. Gaining a clear understanding and breakdown may require a careful and thoughtful analysis. Some common possibilities are listed below:

Start-Up/Mobilization Capital	Funds required to purchase goods and services to launch a business. Purchases typically are one-time in nature and include legal and accounting fees to establish an enterprise, office equipment, and marketing material development.
Working Capital	Cash needed to fund day to day operations including salaries, rent and marketing costs over a period of time, such as a year.
Accounts Receivable	Funds needed as an advance against existing eligible accounts receivable (normally those no more than 90 days due).
Inventory	Funds needed to acquire inventory (including pieces for assembly for future sale).
Equipment	Funds needed for equipment for all aspects of the business, including manufacturing equipment, computers, and copiers.
Real Estate	Funding for acquisition of real estate to be held for business use.
Business Acquisition	Funds used to acquire assets of an existing business. May include funding for inventory, equipment, customer lists and goodwill.

Amount of Financing Required

Once the purpose and type of financing have been identified, the next step is to quantify the amount of money needed. The goal of this process is to enable a prospective financier to arrive at the same conclusion you reached relative to the amount of necessary financing. Of course, the business applicant still has the burden of making a compelling pitch.

At a minimum, a comprehensive cash flow projection should be included to support the amount of financing. Depending on the nature of funding, however, additional transaction-specific cash analyses may be necessary. For example, a summary of average accounts receivable and accounts payable turnover may be appropriate in the case of receivables financing. The illustration on the following page shows a sample cash analysis involving accounts receivables and payables.

In the hypothetical case presented, it is logical to conclude financing in the range of $80,000 ($40,000 month 1 and $40,000 month 2) is needed to pay expenses as they become due.

ACCOUNTS RECEIVABLE FINANCING ANALYSIS			
	Month 1	Month 2	Month 3
Sales – Billings	$100,000	$300,000	$500,000
Collections			
Current	20,000	60,000	100,000
> 30 Days	0	50,000	150,000
> 60 Days	0	0	30,000
> 90 Days	0	0	0
Total Estimated Collections	20,000	$110,000	$280,000
Accounts Payable	$60,000	$180,000	$300,000
Payments			
Current	30,000	90,000	150,000
> 30 Days		30,000	90,000
> 60 Days			
> 90 Days			
Notes Payable	10,000	10,000	10,000
Other	20,000	20,000	30,000
Total Estimated Disbursements	$60,000	$150,000	$260,000
Summary			
Collections	$20,000	$110,000	$280,000
Disbursements	60,000	150,000	260,000
Net Cash from Operations	($40,000)	($40,000)	$20,000

131

SOURCE AND TIMING OF REPAYMENT

A financing proposal should also specify the anticipated time and method of loan repayment or distribution of earnings to investors. Some general guidelines to consider are provided below:

Financing Purpose	Normal Period of Repayment
Start-up/Mobilization Capital	6-24 months
Working Capital	1-5 years
Accounts Receivable	1 year revolving
Inventory	1 year revolving
Equipment	3-7 years
Real Estate	15-25 years
Business Acquisition	5-10 years

Most often companies repay loans from operating profits. For example, cash flow from operations satisfies contract financing, inventory purchases and receivables financing. Monthly cash flow, however, is not the only source of repayment. Be sure to inform your banker or investor if repayment depends on future refinancing or asset sales.

CHOOSING A FINANCIER

People in business should be very selective when choosing a financing partner. Seasoned veterans recognize this relationship essentially is a marriage. By analogy, family and friends would advise proceeding cautiously, and not relying solely on emotion when choosing a mate. Important parallels can be drawn with respect to choosing a financing partner.

An entrepreneur in the start-up stage may desire a fairly personal and consultative financing relationship, especially when the business-

> *In selecting a financing partner, one size does not fit all.*

person has no prior experience. On the other hand, a more mature enterprise with a successful track record may have little or no need to interface with a financier. Many of the practical considerations for selecting a financing partner are listed below:

- Do you need a financier who will provide some technical assistance in addition to funding?

- Do you need a financier who can offer ancillary services, including payroll processing, cash management, lock box, direct deposit or electronic and internet banking services?

- Do you want a personal relationship with one individual who knows, understands and is in regular contact with your business?

- Do you simply want a money exchange whereby funds are available for draw down when needed and repaid as required?

- Do you want a financier that has the capacity to finance your business needs as they evolve in the intermediate and long-term future?

Ideally, most companies start with a short list of financial prospects who match up with their specific needs and requirements. Measuring overall compatibility is the primary objective.

Lenders and venture capitalists tend to specialize in specific industries and industry segments. They also differ along the lines of allowable uses of funds. Some financiers may only advance against accounts receivable, while others depend on tangible personal equipment and commercial real estate. Fortunately, the investment capital community is highly diverse and chances are there is a match for virtually every type of need.

Familiarity with the types and practices of different types of financiers can help expedite the search for an acceptable financing partner. Specifically, knowledge of their particular fields of concentration, underwriting standards and pricing structures can easily separate prospects from suspects. A list and description of the most likely candidates is provided below:

Commercial Banks	Commercial banks typically provide short and medium term debt financing, and business lending usually represents the majority of their loan portfolios. The cost of financing is a function of the prevailing prime rate of interest. Typically loans are priced at two or more points above prime, depending on the overall credit evaluation of the business.
Leasing Companies	Leasing companies provide an alternative to debt and equity financing, especially for equipment. Sometimes leasing is a viable option to purchasing for reasons relating to income taxes, financing restrictions and obsolescence. Leases usually carry a built in or imputed interest factor slightly higher than commercial bank rates.
Factors	Factors are specialized commercial financing companies that make business loans indirectly by purchasing accounts receivable from borrowers. Factors charge a discount rate that equates to interest. The effective cost is a function of prevailing interest rates, the percent of uncollected receivables, and the company's historic performance. Typically factoring is a relatively expensive method of financing.

Venture Capital Funds	Venture capital firms provide equity financing in exchange for a piece of ownership in the company. As a result, venture firms typically are willing to wait longer for their returns than are banking institutions. Funding generally ranges upward from $250,000, and requires 25% to 50% return on their investments each year. Returns can reach 500% over the life of the investment. The terms for financing vary widely among venture capital funds.
Investment Banks	Investment banks help raise capital through public offerings of equity shares and corporate bonds of businesses. Generally, the investment banker assumes responsibility for selling the securities at a set price to the general public. Stock and bond prices depend on both market factors and overall economic conditions. Often stocks provide a dividend payable periodically at the discretion of the board of directors. Bonds offer a stated rate of interest, payable at periodic intervals, set accordingly to the bonds' rating, based on the company's credit history and future projections.
Public and Governmental Financing Programs	There are various federal, state and local government funds to assist business owners. Most funds share the objectives of job retention and new job creation. Some define eligibility by industry, some define it by size. Many funds target businesses which cannot obtain traditional financing from banks. Financial support varies by program and includes grants, direct loans, loan guarantees, contract financing and surety bonding. Ordinarily public and governmental funding involves interest on direct loans, fees on loan guarantees and premiums on surety bonds. The rates vary widely depending on the source, use and term of the financing.

What distinguishes financiers most often is their appetite and preference for certain types of financing. It probably would be an unproductive use of time, for example, to pursue venture capital to finance the purchase of equipment costing $200,000 or less. Similarly, it would be ill advised to place a working capital loan request with a leasing company. On the other hand, an investment bank could be the perfect match for a mature company with a history of stable earnings and desire to go public. Understanding the financiers' appetite will save you valuable time and unnecessary frustration.

MAKING THE CUT

Completing the financing process successfully can be exhausting and time consuming. Even a business with a positive record of earnings generally can expect to encounter some resistance and perhaps some rejections. While financial performance and future prospects weigh heavily, financing request rejections are often precipitated by lack of financial documentation or a lack of clarity about specific financing need.

Sometimes entrepreneurial companies are declined for financing due to lack of reliable company prepared financial statements or an absence of professionally prepared financial statements. Financiers' sometimes complain that their ability to thoroughly and responsibly evaluate revenues and expenses or business assets and liabilities was impaired. Whenever financiers are hampered from performing a complete financial analysis chances of a favorable response to a funding request are slim. Accordingly, appropriate precautions should be taken in advance to ensure financial statements and disclosures are complete and contain no material inaccuracies.

Often times, discrepancies relate to the content and credibility of financial forecasts. For instance, an accompanying cash flow projection may be at odds with historical data, market conditions, industry outlook or the business plan. Financiers will be very skeptical whenever there is a blatant disparity with these critical factors. Remember, your projections and your plan speak volumes about your company. For the most part, you only have one opportunity to make a good first impression.

Key assumptions underlying financial forecasts must be intact as well. Lack of back up for pivotal figures in the forecast is a "no-no." Assumptions should be explained and reasonably reflect market indicators, surveys, contracts or other metrics.

Other negatives that derail financing proposals include overly optimistic or weak revenue and earnings estimates. Your revenue estimates should be reasonably consistent with both historical financial performance and prevailing market conditions. Major departures should be explained thoroughly. Atypical estimated spikes in revenue sometimes serve more to raise serious concerns about the creditability of the financial forecast than they address. By way of example, a revenue forecast that puts next year's revenue at $1,000,000 while the average for the prior three years was less than $500,000 will most assuredly cause trepidation.

Most financiers rely on various tangible and intangible factors in approving or rejecting an investment opportunity.

Finally, bankers and investors will be inclined to pass on deals where projected operating expenses appear unreasonably low. For instance, a projection in which sales are estimated to increase more than 30% but operating and overhead expenses remain flat should also cause a potential lender to doubt reasonableness.

Designing a Dossier

Figuratively speaking, a financing dossier should always be carried in a CEO's hip pocket. To be prepared to negotiate with prospective financiers for growth and expansion capital, entrepreneurs must be in position to supply the basic financial information needed for review and evaluation on an expedited basis.

A financing dossier should contain the most common records, documents and financial disclosures that virtually any credible investor or lender would request. Savvy entrepreneurs have a financing dossier accessible and ready for circulation in quick order. They treat this document like a personal resume; everyone needs to keep one handy and keep it updated.

A guide for contents is available online through the auspices of various financing groups and institutions. Most financing institutions and private capital sources subscribe to a common list of document requirements. Standard items are listed below:

- Overview of the business model

- Summary of the relevant industry and market

- Description of core competencies or areas of specialization

- Resumes of owners and key management

- Corporate documents, including articles of incorporation, partnership agreements, and by-laws

- Company financial statements for most recent three years

- Monthly cash flow projection for two years and summary of critical assumptions underlying the projections

- Statement of proposed uses of funds

- Summary of existing business debt and copies of loan documents

- Business leases or deeds

- Description and value of collateral

- Current personal financial statements for all owners

- Current credit report for business, if available; if not, current credit reports for all owners

- Personal tax returns for prior three years for principal business owners

In addition to developing a comprehensive dossier you must shop for prospective financiers with compatible underwriting guidelines. The criteria below is representative of the way some of the most sophisticated private lenders explain their areas of interest.

UNDERWRITING GUIDELINES	
Industry Preferences	• Computer and Information Services • Health Care Services • Communications
Investment Size	• $500,000 to $1,500,000
Investment Vehicles	• Senior debt with or without equity conversion features • Subordinated or mezzanine debt • Participating and convertible preferred stock • Common stock
Geographic Preferences	• Mid-Atlantic Region

Other Criteria	• Identified viable marketplace niche • Strong management with proven track record • Potential to generate substantial economic activity in the minority community • Potential to provide generous return on investment[2]

For the various reasons discussed in this chapter it is essential for entrepreneurs to do their homework prior to submitting a request for funding. The most streamline presentation with accompanying supporting documentation is most likely to garner a positive response.

NOTABLE REFLECTIONS AT A GLANCE

→ Financing alternatives should be assessed strategically.

→ Quantify financing needs from the start.

→ Advantages and disadvantages of equity and debt should be weighed on a case-by-case basis.

→ Selection of a compatible financing partner is key to a productive financing relationship.

→ Lenders and investors will monitor business progress to protect funds they place at risk.

→ The profile of financing needs and objectives must match the underwriting criteria of the perspective financier.

→ An up-to-date financing dozier should be maintained on file.

CHAPTER EIGHT
Inspect What You Expect...
Instill Peak Performance

| *Journey* |

BJ shared his concerns regarding Matrix's future profitability with his accountant, Mitchell Ryan and expected to receive positive feedback after discussing his plans to diversify into the technology side of the industry. Much to BJ's surprise, Mitchell was not enthusiastic.

Mitchell suggested BJ more fully analyze the causes of Matrix's declining rate of profits before committing to this new path. He cautioned that weak financial controls could be at the root of the unfavorable earnings trend, and if so any financial dysfunctions would be compounded with diversification and growth. As such, Mitchell encouraged BJ to evaluate the quality of his company's financial checks and balances.

BJ admitted to Mitchell that as the business had matured he had become far less involved in supervising and directing daily financial activities. He confessed that in recent years his priority had been sales growth. Recognizing his own shortsightedness, BJ plans to take a more active role in managing the financial side of the business and enhance his company's financial controls. He wants to start by examining operating and administrative functions of the business most critical to production of earnings.

Imagine, at last, your business has successfully secured long sought capital. However, in the face of this major triumph your jubilance is tempered by high anxiety over future performance. Deep down you still wonder whether your projections are too optimistic. There is real concern that profits may fall far short of expectation. Ultimately the final outcome will hinge on productivity, efficiency and cost control.

Just like BJ, entrepreneurs on the rise often entertain second thoughts about being able to deliver on their promises. The key to achieving projected performance usually lies in managing pivotal cost factors; such as labor, materials and other expenditures required to make finished products and services. Effective management of these variables requires becoming adept at manufacturing your product or service with maximum efficiency.

Performance management can be a daunting challenge unless you have well designed control systems. Too often leaders in business are caught off guard when the quality of operations begin to deteriorate in the face of increasing sales growth. They fail to realize growth sometimes produces anomalies, that is, higher growth may breed lower productivity.

Promoting efficiency starts with day-to-day oversight of operating activities. Specifically, who does what, when, and at what cost. There are several ways to evaluate the alignment financially, namely, through benchmarking, performance measures and budgeting. Each method will be discussed in this chapter. Suffice to say, during periods of intense growth these methods are crucial to employ just to stay on track.

Are you convinced your performance management approach will support profitability and productivity if your sales goals are realized? Truth is, absent a solid performance oversight plan, operations may slide backward in terms of output, quality and profit. Accordingly, the objective of this chapter is to review performance management tools and techniques.

CHAPTER HIGHLIGHTS:

→ Financial Drivers

→ Performance Oversight

→ Streamline Budgeting

→ Trouble Shooting

→ Benchmarking

THE "X" FACTORS

A pre-requisite for maximizing financial returns is strong performance management and oversight. Keeping an eye on what I call the X factors will test your tolerance. A few key working components of a business have the potential to dramatically impact efficiency and in turn cash flow and profitability upward or downward.

Because X factors play an integral role in determining the bottom line, they have to be closely monitored and choreographed. This means entrepreneurs must become well-acquainted with the normal patterns of behavior associated with each X factor.

At the most basic level, performance-driven businesses focus on fine tuning work their administrative and operating flow process. They routinely work to eliminate billing, log jams, production back-up, employee absenteeism, unnecessary overtime pay, and chronic machine breakdowns. These types of problems cause bottlenecks that drag down productivity, cash flow and profitability. Fortunately, there are a handful of basic tools and strategies that will help alleviate these problems.

A simple but highly useful tool that will help weed out inefficiency is a budget. When thoughtfully and meticulously developed, a budget promotes production efficiency by tracking activity by units of input and output.

A key planning technique that assists in estimating dollar costs is known as an "Activity Budget." The focal point of an activity budget are X factors, that is, those activities that are subject to change and stifle efficiency.

Without an activity budget most CEO's would be at a loss to estimate the dollar cost of labor materials and overhead without a schematic of planned activities. Having a mechanism to register expectations daily, weekly, monthly or on an annual basis is crucial. Finally, to make sense of it all, you will also need to clock actual performance and compare it to budget estimates. These comparisons provide feedback essential for sound planning and budgeting in the future.

A sample activity budget for Potomac LLC, a service enterprise from the case study, is presented on the following page.

There are many different formats that will effectively diagram significant operating activities tied to productivity. The key to constructing a design that will help both monitor and evaluate behavior. Poor performance trends may be indicative of bad decisions, unfavor-

ACTIVITY BUDGET

Potomac, LLC

Review of Operations

	Past Week			This Month			Year-to-Date		
	Budget	Actual	Variance	Budget	Actual	Variance	Budget	Actual	Variance
Production:									
Labor Hrs – Regular	600	645	45	2,400	2,560	160	7,200	7,500	300
Labor Hrs – Overtime	40	40	-	20	65	45	60	155	95
Employee Training	20	20	-	100	100	-	200	200	-
Shipments:									
Gross Shipments	8K	12.5K	4.5K	450K	360K	(90K)	2.5K	2.25K	250
Delivery Returns	5	6	1	20	14	-6	35	32	-3
Reworks:									
New Accounts	1	-	-1	4	3	-1	15	13	-2
Old Accounts	-	1	1	3	4	1	10	12	2
Internal Audits:									
Main Office	-	2	2	10	15	5	25	30	5
Field Offices	-	4	4	4	8	4	15	28	13

able conditions, or a combination thereof. In the end, when it comes to sorting out problem areas an activity budget should make the job much easier.

Regular reporting is especially important so that managers and supervisors are able to keep productivity in check. Budget tools should empower staff up and down the line to regulate performance and institute appropriate measures for maximizing efficiency. Organizations typically perform best where staff evaluate pathways for better performance and take more ownership in performance outcomes.

Generally speaking, activity-based budgeting is adaptable for businesses engaged in fabrication, assembly and production where operations involve processing. Likewise, many fast food chains will find the approach effective in monitoring daily operations, especially where fluctuations in labor costs and inventory purchasing are closely tied to sales.

Surprisingly, activity budgeting also plays a major role in enhancing productivity in service enterprises as well. They too must overcome struggles to maximize and supervise work flow efficiency and productivity. Financial advisors generally regard activity budgeting as a prerequisite for businesses to realize a healthy bottom line.

PRIME FINANCIAL DRIVERS

In addition to smoothing over workflow for maximum efficiency and productivity, CEOs should always keep in sight operating and administrative processes that bear the greatest impact on the bottom line. I refer to this subset of X factors as "financial drivers."

Maintaining a firm handle on financial drivers should be job one for CEOs and key decision makers. To achieve best performance, they must maintain close watch over matters of financial significance and pose the most risk for cost overruns . Similarly, management must look to scan financial drivers for opportunities to elevate net earnings. The oversight function not only begs for direct involvement and leadership but day-to-day guidance and direction.

In managing profits, entrepreneurs, CEOs and high level managers do not have the luxury of being a bystander. Out of necessity they have to be closely involved just to help decide what buttons to push and where to channel productive resources.

A misguided focus could be fatal. For example, a CEO of a growing company that spends most of his or her time in marketing but fails to notice a gapping hole in purchasing and inventory control may be setting their company up for a string of operating losses. On the other hand, production flow may be top notch but customer deliveries are chronically late and result in a relatively high rate of cancellations and loss of sales.

Moreover, it is critical to know, understand and prioritize your financial drivers. At various times and stages of business development, your assessments are bound to change. For this reason intuition alone should not be relied upon to tell the whole story or keep you ahead of the game.

A simple weighted ranking system may help to set the proper balance. Conceptually, you and your management team might pick out roughly fifteen key activities to assign an impact ranking from highest to lowest. A sample illustration of a ranking grid using Matrix from the case study is illustrated on the following page.

MATRIX, INC. PROFIT AND CASH FLOW PERFORMANCE WATCH LIST			
Operational Components	Weight (1=Low Impact 15=High Impact)		
	Profit	Cash	Total
Pricing/Billing/Discounting	12	11	23
Product Mix/Sales Volume	15	15	30
Proposals/Bidding/Contract Negotiation	9	7	16
Labor Hours/Rates/Benefits	2	2	4
Staff Recruitment/Training/Retention	12	12	24
Selling Incentives/Sales Reps/Commissions	11	6	17
Locations/No. of Stores/No. of Offices	8	4	12
Advertising/Media Promotions	5	5	10
Vendor Selection/Supplier Pricing/Credit Terms	13	9	22
Project Management/Supervision	4	4	8
Documentation/Billing/Collections	6	10	16
Intellectual Property/Licensing	3	3	6
Transportation/Shipping & Delivery	14	14	28
Technology/Systems/Communications	10	8	18
Financing Costs/Interest/Lease Rates	7	12	19

According to the ranking above the top five drivers for Matrix in order of importance are as follows:

1. Product Mix/Sales Volume

2. Transportation/Shipping & Delivery

3. Staff Recruitment/Training/Retention

4. Pricing/Discounting

5. Vendor Selection/ Supplier Pricing/Credit Terms

Regardless of size or industry maintaining a positive bottom line will be tied to how well financial drivers are both identified, understood and managed. To keep performance in the high range, your management team must continually re-evaluate and reassess different financial drivers. Also, when necessary even you as CEO should be prepared to micro-manage key financial drivers.

SIMPLIFYING BUSINESS ECONOMICS

Financial drivers bear a very close relationship to profit and loss.

A set of sound economic principles also lie at the core of every high performing business. Essentially, your fundamental economic model for success has to be imbedded in routine business policies and practices. Many basic principles are familiar and exercised by people in everyday life. For example, don't spend every dollar you make; don't be pennywise and dollar foolish; and try not to live above your means. Most of us are keenly aware of these gems of wisdom although we don't always follow them.

Likewise, in the business world there are at least a dozen basic economic feats that are universally recognized. They speak to when, where and how to manage business resources. The chart below highlights some of these important fundamentals:

Most any plan devised to enhance productivity and minimize costs will draw from a combination of the simple guidelines highlighted above. Too often, businesses neglect to think about these percepts when formulating major plans and strategies. As a result, financial performance is lackluster at best.

PRODUCTIVITY

Work Flow Efficiency = Higher Employee Productivity

Job Training = Reduced Error Rate and Higher Output

Equipment Upgrade or Replacement = Less Downtime and Increased Production

Temporary Labor = Avoid Disruption and Maintain Output Levels

COST CONTROL

Competitive Bidding = Lower Prices

Periodic Inventories = Improved Accountability and Asset Protection

Waste Controls and Recycling = Lower Unit Cost

Shipping & Storage = Lower Carrier and Space Costs

Quality Management = Minimizes Customer Returns

Outsourcing=Cost Savings

PROFIT AND CASH FLOW

Sales Growth = Higher Income and Added Cash Flow

Production Unit Costing = Profit Margin Control and Management

Receivables Collection = Accelerated Cash Flow and Lower Level of Financing

Spending Limits = Built-In Spending Control

Financial Audit = Heightened Financial Compliance and Objectivity

Benchmarking Best Practices

Even when a business is convinced of its superior performance, it will not hurt to put its best to a test. It is only human nature to relax over time and sometimes, trend backwards.

An objective approach for routinely evaluating your company's performance is advised. A growing number of companies rely on a relatively simple method known as "benchmarking." This technique basically gathers for comparison the best information available from as many credible sources as possible, both within and outside the business. Then, the methods used by compatible high achievers are systematically implemented.

Benchmarking guards against the false assumption that operational performance is ideal. It relies extensively on outside external comparisons to validate internal assumptions. For instance, a retail business may decide to set benchmarks based on companies that achieve superior in-store sales at minimum cost; or which are widely known for exceptional customer satisfaction. For example, these companies may be inclined to look to Apple Computers and Trader Joe's:

• Apple's retail stores recently reported annual revenue per square foot of $4,032, exceeding sales per square foot of such notable stores as Neiman Marcus, Best Buy and Tiffany's. Red Herring defined Apple's recipe for success:

> *Unlike its rivals, Apple gives customers instant gratification by keeping inventory in stores. The company has opened stores slowly, building up anticipation for its stores. Finally, those stores are some of the tiniest in retail – encouraging customers to*

drop far more money than they might in a dusty computer shop or utilitarian web site. [1]

- Trader Joe's is widely acclaimed for its customer friendly focus. Fast Company summarizes the company's approach.

Trader Joe's business model allows it to respond to customer feedback in ways that other supermarkets cannot. Suppliers do not pay fees, or "rent," to place products on Trader Joe's shelves, a widespread industry practice that's anything but customer-focused. With drastically smaller square footage and inventories than typical grocery stores, the company removes items that don't sell well to make room for new products. In a sense, Trader Joe's entire inventory is a result of listening to customers – both their feedback and their dollars. [2]

Benchmarking is not only germane to retail merchandising and manufacturing but also for service enterprises. Service enterprises are also adopting benchmarking to promote greater efficiency and higher productivity. As stated in The McKinsey Quarterly,

For service businesses of nearly every stripe, particularly in North America and Europe, manufacturing provides a glimpse into the future. Under unrelenting competitive pressure, they are reexamining the role of operations in creating competitive advantage and asking themselves which clearly differentiated services they can provide and how they can deliver those services to customers as efficiently as possible – and more effectively than their rivals do. Today's leading industrial companies asked and answered similar questions two decades ago, and many executives of service companies now believe that they can adopt the methodologies and tools that have already transformed manufacturers. [3]

Claude Brunet, AXA Insurance company management-board member confirmed this trend. "We are using approaches that have worked very effectively at manufacturing companies and adapting them to our environment. These approaches include... benchmarking costs among AXA companies." [4]

Lastly, numerous government agencies have implemented benchmarking as a management tool as well. For example, the Customs-Trade Partnership Against Terrorism, a strategic alliance between U.S. Customs and Border Protection and major U.S. importers, has defined best practices in supply chain security to protect from concealment of terrorist weapons in imports. [5]

When it comes to best practices it is not always necessary to reinvent the wheel. Many techniques employed by very successful companies are available in the public domain for use in formulating better business practices.

LEVERAGING BUDGET FORECASTS

Many people in business confess boredom, if not apathy, at the notion of financial budgeting. The tendency in many businesses is to marginalize and undervalue the budget process and its significance to profitability. On the contrary, a well-planned budget is the best way to leverage your financial resources and thereby maximize earnings.

Many times, the advantage that one business enjoys over another rests solely with superior cost management and control. Companies that master the art of finan-

> *The tendency is to marginalize and undervalue the budget process and its significance to profitability.*

cial budgeting normally dictate competitive pricing and operating cost advantages in their particular industry.

> *Benchmarking guards against the false assumption that operational performance is where it should be.*

The development of an activity budget is key to devising a reliable financial budget. In essence, the schedule of planned activity is a guidepost for estimating financial expenditures. At the end of the day, you should aim to translate activities and key assumptions based on the planned work flow into a monetary forecast.

The monthly, quarterly and annual financial budget is essential for cost management. Without a financial point of reference the consumption or purchase price of raw material, merchandise, and services may increase substantially without your knowledge. For example, a major supplier could begin passing along added costs and surcharges. Needless to say without financial measures, these and other significant cost changes may go undetected until the bottom line is irreversibly damaged.

Sound financial budgeting is indeed the backbone of a performance driven enterprise. Whether a business is centralized or decentralized, a tightly knitted budget will be invaluable from the standpoint of financial discipline and accountability. This practice will also help establish incentive based compensation.

A chief decision-maker should never make the mistake of assuming the responsibility for financial budgeting falls strictly in their accountant's domain. Whether choosing the format, frequency of reporting or key financial assumptions upper management should always be intricately engaged in the budget process.

In a rapidly changing economy, even a business in a vibrant industry, cannot take future profitability for granted. They too need a detailed blueprint to guide performance. Such built-in controls enhance the ability of a business to perpetuate success year after year.

> *Sound financial budgeting is the backbone of a performance driven enterprise.*

TROUBLE-SHOOTING TIDBITS

A reliable cost control system provides the best means of spotting trouble early enough to prevent major harm. As reports are scrutinized, attention will naturally be drawn to unusual variations. The key is to develop a system that will readily flag latent problems.

The financial budget should be looked at as an instrument for alerting senior management to operating and financial malfunctions. The behavior of actual costs in relation to specific budget line items should be analyzed in depth. The following parameters may be most telling:

- Line item expense as a percent of revenues

- Net income as a percent of gross sales

- Labor hours in comparison to production

- Cost of goods as percent of gross sales

- Sales potential based on production

The amounts reflected in the budget represent check points for maintaining a profitable operation. To help facilitate the investigative process, most operating budgets report three columnar amounts: budget, actual, and variance. In most instances every "variance" will be a reflection of your business practices and strategies whether positive or negative.

Another lifeline for management to use for trouble shooting purposes are the assumptions underlying the various budget estimates. Because of their importance, key assumptions should always be spelled out in writing. This will enable each operating unit, department and staff person involved to look back after the fact and determine where things may have gone.

It is also analytically helpful when the line items in the financial budget mirror the chart of accounts used for accounting purposes. The chart of accounts is a descriptive list of account titles used for accumulating financial activity to be reported in the financial statements. Ideally, it should be relatively easy to compare budgets and financial statements.

A streamline illustration of a financial budget for Matrix featuring the qualities described is presented below:

MATRIX, INC. FINANCIAL BUDGET ($000 OMITTED)			
	Actual	Budget	Variance
Revenues			
Maintenance	$10,500	$11,250	-750
Hospitality	26,000	23,750	2,250
	36,500	35,000	1,500
Cost of Goods Sold			
Maintenance Products	$7,350	$6,950	($400)
Hospitality Products	16,900	16,000	-900
	24,250	22,950	-1300
Gross Profit	$12,250	$12,050	$200
Selling and Operating Expenses	10,420	10,000	-420
Net Income (Loss)	$1,830	$2,050	($220)

A quick glance of the budget report provides a view of major variances between budget and actual performance.

- Sales of maintenance products were $750,000 under budget, while hospitality products were $2,250,000 ahead of projection.

- For hospitality, inventory purchases classified as "cost of goods sold" exceeded budget by $900,000, and the maintenance division was also over budget by $400,000.

- Overall net income (gross profit less selling and operating expenses) was $220,000 unfavorable compared to budget.

A progressive management team would be inclined to investigate and analyze the favorable or unfavorable reasons behind the differences shown.

NAILING DOWN OUTLIERS

From a financial standpoint, when you are running a business it is extremely important to understand cause and effect. For this reason, performance-driven companies strive to pinpoint and then nail down budget outliers. Determining the cause for any major variances should almost always be given a very high priority.

A simple way to decipher cause is to extend the analysis of budget variances to their most likely sources. Usually the culprit lies in greater or lesser usage or price than was budgeted.

Determining the causes for significant budget variances should be given a high priority.

The normal pattern can be demonstrated from the prior illustration involving Matrix. A main cost area that prevented the company from maximizing earnings was cost of goods. The maintenance division was unfavorable by $400,000. To get to the underlying causes, the following analysis of usage and price could be performed.

	Budget Price	Budget Quantity	Combined Total
MATRIX, INC.			
VARIANCE ANALYSIS			
Maintenance:			
Cleaning Detergent -- Budget	$5.00 / gal.	1,390,000 gals.	$6,950,000
Price Variance:			
Actual Price	$5.00 / gal.		
- Budgeted Price	$4.75/ gal.		
Difference	$0.25 / gal.		
X Budgeted Quantity	1,390,000 gals.		
Price Variance	$347,500		
- Unfavorable			
Volume Variance:			
Actual Quantity		1,400,500 gals.	
- Budgeted Quantity		1,390,000 gals.	
Difference		10,500 gals.	
x Budgeted Price		$5 / gal.	
Volume (usage) Variance		$52,500	
- Unfavorable			
Recap of Total Budget Variance:			
Price Variance		$347,500	
Volume Variance		52,500	
Total Budget Varience			400,000
Actual Cost			$7,350,000

The analysis above indicates that Matrix experienced a significant budget variance in cost of goods sold attributed to an unfavorable price reduction of $.25 per gallon totaling in aggregate, $347,500. Likewise, the usage of detergent was over budget by 10,400 gallons resulting in $52,500 unfavorable variance. A combination of the two overages resulted in a $400,000 unfavorable variance.

As the CEO of Matrix, you might ask: "Was the price increase avoidable by switching suppliers; or was the use of detergents wasteful?" In the final analysis, you would want to determine whether the overages were within the control of your managers and supervisors. A general guide for determining the influence of price and usage variances is provided below.

Price Variance = (Actual Price – Budget Price) x Budgeted Volume

Measures the variance in revenues or expenses resulting from the difference between the budgeted average price per unit sold or purchased and the realized actual price.

Volume Variance = (Actual Volume – Budget Volume) x Budgeted Price

Measures the variance in revenues or expenses resulting from the difference between the budgeted and the realized volume of activity.

NOTABLE REFLECTIONS AT A GLANCE

→ Budget anticipated expenditure of funds associated with producing products or rendering services.

→ Take time to translate assigned performance expectations to various operating units, departments and staff.

→ Use a variance analysis to lead an investigation into fall offs in productivity and profitability.

→ Oversee dominant financial drivers to insure peak performance.

→ Treat performance oversight as a work in progress.

CHAPTER NINE
Lock Down Prosperity...
Tighten Up Legally

| *The Journey* |

After much deliberation, BJ has decided diversification would be the most effective way to protect market share and profits in the future. Convinced the best opportunity for growth could be in customizing technology solutions for inventory control and distribution, he decided to launch a new technology venture.

Ambition did not cloud his sense of reasoning. BJ recognized he would not be the ideal person to manage technical operations within an IT company. Accordingly, he asked his good friend Taylor who has the technical expertise to consider teaming up, and to his great pleasure, Taylor responded enthusiastically to the overture.

The friends recognized that many decisions had been made regarding their business relationship from the outset of their discussion. However, they still must agree upon the type of legal entity. Alternatives include a joint venture, merger or subcontracting relationship. Taylor opposed forming a corporation, in favor of a limited liability company and BJ, less concerned about choice of entity was eager to decide their respective investment contribution and share of profit and loss.

The pair agreed $300,000 was the magic number necessary to mobilize operations. They anticipate the bulk of funds will be used for start up costs, including working capital, marketing and business development. The remainder will be necessary to purchase various computer equipment, accessories, and software.

To Taylor's chagrin, BJ also insisted on a buy-sell agreement. He felt it would be invaluable, should either he or Taylor need to withdraw from the business due to disability, death, or personal reasons.

If you are like most entrepreneurs, when you started or expanded your business you rushed into a legal structure without completely understanding the legal ramifications and distinctions. Many times, business people simply make a selection solely based on what they learned from a layman rather than on the advice of a professional.

The potential of being saddled with legal liability in excess of business insurance is a serious enough threat to get every business owner's attention. In case of legal liability, a judgment creditor may first look to be paid from insurance, thereafter turn to business assets and if still not fully compensated, to the personal assets of business owners to the extent the may be legally accessible.

In business, just focusing on making money to the exclusion of asset protection would be a big mistake. A key to longevity and stability is securing the legal interest of stakeholders. In absence of adequate safeguards confusion, disputes and strife from both internal and external sources can cause business demise. This usually translates to needless consumption of time and resources at a very hefty price.

Unless the friends and colleagues who advised you early on were business lawyers, a fresh evaluation of the legal status of your business is probably in order. This chapter will serve to provide some basic considerations to get you started.

CHAPTER HIGHLIGHTS:

→ Asset Protection

→ Choice of Business Entity

→ Teaming Alternatives

→ Buy-Sell Arrangements

→ Proactive Legal Practices

KEY FOCUS AREAS

Prior to launching a promising business venture it is wise to first address the issue of asset protection. In most cases this involves establishing a separate legal identity. This rule of thumb is not only sound advice for new companies, but for established businesses as well especially when considering an unrelated or distinct new line of product or service.

By custom, many large businesses establish multiple companies; typically with several subsidiaries under the parent. Frequently, the reason for carving up a conglomerate into separate legal parts is to minimize risk of loss. Ideally to the extent possible, profit making divisions should be protected from the failure of a start-up or expansion.

Investors in one business venture simply may not wish to participate financially in unrelated or new activities of an existing company. In some instances investors will only make a capital contribution if their investment is housed in a legal entity that is separate and distinct.

On the other hand, legal structure is driven by a desire for protection against personal liability. Most principal business owners are unwilling to expose their residence, personal savings, investment property, securities and other assets to debts of a business. In essence, stakeholders strive to restrict any personal exposure for legal damages to their financial investment.

From a strategic perspective an entrepreneur may wish to segregate one business operation from another especially where significant intangible value already exist in terms of goodwill, reputation and customer base.

Preserving intangible assets is yet another conceivable reason to take special legal measures for asset protection. For example, a start-up could place in jeopardy a mature business that already possesses substantial goodwill, reputation and customer base. In that case, setting up another separate legal business to operate an upstart may be prudent.

Last but not least, sometimes for strategic reasons business owners choose to enter teaming relationships to spark growth and expansion. However, even in a solid joint venture written agreements establishing a separate identity should still be the first order of business to protect the interests of all partners.

Limiting Investor Liability

Most important, a separate legal identity offers the all important advantage of "limited legal liability." In essence, this offers a means of asset protection that will extend to principal owners as well as outside investors. Also, the extent of investor exposure to creditors will be minimized.

Fortunately, there are a variety of ways to structure a business so as to provide limited legal liability. However, while incorporating raises the threshold of limited liability, many entrepreneurs fail to realize that even with incorporations, no business is completely risk free legally speaking.

In legal battles where a business is the defendant, an aggrieved party may argue in court that an entity's "corporate veil" should be pierced, especially when the company itself lacks sufficient resources to pay the judgment. In other words, the plaintiff could ask the court to waive the cloak of limited liability accorded by the legal form of business. Sometimes, your best legal argument rests in a history of operating the business legally in a manner compliant and consistent with applicable legal requirements and customs of an incorporated business.

Most courts will dismiss pleas to pierce the corporate veil unless an incorporated business has failed to follow appropriate legal practices and customs many of which will be highlighted later in this chapter. When courts do consider lifting the veil of protection, those who actively participate in management are also vulnerable.

With these risks in mind, every business owner should become be familiar with certain basic do's and don'ts. For instance, in virtually every instance owners of a separate legal entity should avoid commingling their personal and business finances. Whenever personal and business funds flow through the same bank account courts may be more inclined to consider the owner and business a single combined operating unit for purposes of liability. For this reason, combining cash deposits and disbursements in a single bank account is a "no no."

> *To preserve limited liability protection, owners of a separate legal entity should avoid commingling their personal and business finances.*

It is advisable to comply with established formalities for legal forms of business organization. For instance, in some jurisdictions corporations whether large or small are required by regulation to conduct a formal meeting of the shareholders and directors at least once annually. For major decisions such as merger, consolidation, sale of assets or dissolution a formal recording also may need to be made. These legal peculiarities make a compelling case for seeking the advice of an attorney rather than operating simply on one's own intuition.

THE FLASH POINT

To bring more reality to the hazards of personal liability consider this straight forward hypothetical. A friend of yours establishes a wholesale distribution business as a sole proprietorship with an investment of $40,000. Anxious to gain a major new customer, she accepts a sales order within the first week.

Two months afterwards, the wheels start to come off. Your friend's company was unable to deliver the product. Unfortunately, the overseas manufacturer got behind schedule due to a production backlog. This whole predicament left your friend in a "Catch 22," both unable to meet the demands of the customer and unable to force the supplier to deliver.

Assume there was no written agreement specifying conditions of performance and that your friend's business was unincorporated. In the worst case scenario customer is awarded legal damages of $100,000.

As demonstrated in the chart on the following page, your friend's personal net worth would be tapped to the tune of $60,000

Legal forms of business organization provide asset protection for business owners.

in the absence of incorporation. Her personal net worth would drop from $200K to $140K. Suffice it to say, the legal perils of faulty legal handiwork far outweigh the cost of diligent coverage.

A sound legal structure takes on even higher significance in inherently dangerous industries. Companies at the high end of the risk curve include demolition, excavation and construction businesses. However, even in industries that might otherwise appear to be least at risk, dangers of liability lurk. Claims for wrongful employee discharge, negligence, and breach of contract are just a few of the types of employer liabilities that can crop up.

Litigation risks vary from one business to another, but be assured all businesses operate at some level of exposure. Accordingly, proper legal formation and maintenance of a business organization should be a high priority.

BUSINESS BALANCE SHEET			CEO's PERSONAL BALANCE SHEET		
	Before	After		Before	After
Assets:			**Assets:**		
Cash in Bank	$30,000	$30,000	Cash & Investments	$50,000	$50,000
Equipment	20,000	20,000	Investment in Business	40,000	40,000
			Real Estate	300,000	300,000
Total	$50,000	$50,000	Total	$390,000	$390,000
Liabilities:			**Liabilities:**		
Legal Liability	$ -----	$100,000	Personal Legal Liability	$ -----	$60,000
Notes Payable	10,000	10,000	Auto & Consumer Debts	25,000	25,000
			Mortgage	175,000	175,000
Net Worth	40,000	-60,000	Net Worth	200,000	140,000
Total	$50,000	$50,000	Total	$390,000	$390,000

Molding New Companies

When establishing a new venture or separating a division into a distinct company, the main legal objective is to select the most appropriate type of legal entity for the new company. This decision is critical not only in terms of business management and ownership structure but from the standpoint of applicable laws and regulations. Accordingly, a final determination should only be made after consulting professional business and legal advisors.

For the most part, state laws make it relatively simple for businesses of all sizes to incorporate as a limited liability company or corporation. LLCs or corporations are usually available for single-owner business ventures. Therefore, budding entrepreneurs should never rule out incorporation because they happen to be a sole owner.

Single ownership aside, the corporate form of business may be most suitable where numerous investors are involved. The structure promotes centralized management, that is, control exercisable by a few on behalf of many. Corporate directors oversee the business from a policy perspective and appoint officers to manage day-to-day business affairs.

In addition to providing a layer of asset protection, corporations and limited liability companies offer a convenient way to divide and transfer ownership interest to other people.

In large part, the operating template for a corporation is provided by law. Most State laws set specific boundaries for voting rights of shareholders, powers exercisable by the board of directors and executive officers. Even the frequency of shareholder and board meetings is prescribed by law in some jurisdictions.

169

Mature businesses may find it advantageous to change legal entity.

Alternatively, a limited liability company (LLC) may be more compatible for an association of a small number of owners and investors. For the most part, the LLCs are more flexible than their corporate counterpart in terms of standard procedures and protocols. For example, owners or members of limited liability companies are allowed to customize their business relationships in terms of distribution of ownership, method of sharing of profits and losses and division of management authority. In essence, the desires and needs of owners can be more easily introduced into the legal structure.

Start-ups are not alone in the quest to select a compatible legal form of business. Mature businesses sometimes find it more advantageous to change legal entity. The decision may be motivated by changes in ownership or new tax

In some states under common law, failure to renew a business license or pay annual state and local taxes may result in forfeiture of status as a limited liability company or corporation.

laws. For this reason, it is wise to re-evaluate your legal entity at least once every three years.

THE SLIPPERY SLOPE

Even with an understanding of the legal advantages of limited liability a surprising number of entrepreneurs fail to maintain the "good standing" status for their legal entity. One might ask, why an entrepreneur would allow their business to fall out of compliance?

Many times, failure to comply is by default. For example, some entrepreneurs haphazardly discover the status of their corporation or limited liability company was suspended or cancelled. According to some state laws, failure to renew a business license or pay annual state and local taxes may result in forfeiture of status as a limited liability company or

> *The mere undertaking of an activity or association for profit may be legally sufficient to constitute a sole proprietorship or partnership.*

corporation. When this happens, by operation of law a business may revert back to sole proprietorship and general partnerships with no limited liability protection.

In some instances, sole proprietorships and general partnership may be deemed to have been created legally based on the conduct of the people involved. Generally, under common law, whenever a person or persons pursue an activity for profit they may be considered a business operator. This can be a major shock to people who never explicitly agreed to enter business as partners. Consequently, whenever you think to be engaged in a business association it pays to seek competent legal counsel about your choice of legal entity.

TIES THAT BIND

Many businesses discover the most economical and strategic way to grow market share is by teaming up with another business. For many early stage and mature businesses this strategy has proven to be highly effective. Advantages include a chance to accelerate sales growth, secure financing, or gain access to a large customer base. Many Fortune 500 companies routinely target for acquisition companies with a wide distribution, substantial customer base or with specialized technology.

However, it is unwise to form a team without a written agreement. Needless to say, verbal arrangements are highly susceptible to misinterpretation and can lead

> *Reasons to seek a teaming relationship may be both strategic and financial in nature.*

to protracted and costly litigation. Accordingly, a teaming relationship should be well-documented. Defining the key parameters of the business relationship adds value and legal substance to any business association.

Under certain circumstances, it may be advantageous for long-time competitors or suppliers to consider combining forces. Collectively they could gain market share. Alternatively, one party may possess excess capacity or technical expertise that the other could use productively. Consolidation could also help eliminate duplicate administrative and overhead expenses. In the end, entering into a teaming agreement may be economical and cost effective for both companies.

Some of the most common templates for teaming include the following:

JOINT VENTURE

A joint venture is a legal business association between two or more companies. Usually this type of association is narrowly defined to cover a specific business opportunity or undertaking. The joint venture agreement sets terms and conditions of the business relationship in terms of capital investment requirements, duration, and split of profit and loss. Stipulations regarding management authority and the decision making process are also spelled out.

Merger or Consolidation

A merger or consolidation between two companies is generally much more encompassing legally than a joint venture. In essence, a merger or consideration is the equivalent of a full blown marriage between two separate businesses. From a legal perspective, one or both of the businesses involved will lose its identity and become a single entity legally and financially. Assets, liabilities, ownership rights and obligations are pooled under one roof.

Subcontracting

Subcontracting is probably the most common form of a legal teaming relationship. Typically subcontracting is involved when one company decides to hire another to perform specific work requirements for a customer. As opposed to a joint venture or merger there is no real partnership per se. The subcontractor usually simply agrees to complete the assigned work for a specific price. In this instance, the prime contractor is like a broker. They have two legal obligations – to fulfill an agreement between them and their customer and do the same with regard to the subcontractor.

Selecting a compatible teaming model is the equivalent of selecting a legal entity. In both cases, care should be exercised and professional legal advice should be sought.

PRESERVING HARMONY

Absent a comprehensive agreement among and between owners and investors, most businesses would be susceptible to abrupt break-ups and battles. Too often, the dissolution of private businesses occur because owners fail to take time to draft a written agreement covering their business relationship. At great risk legally, founding members often rely solely on trust. Naively, they believe their mutual admiration, respect and friendship will endure no matter what. Unfortunately, history has shown otherwise.

> *Naively, close partners and associates believe their mutual admiration, respect and friendship will endure no matter what.*

The best way to head off internal turmoil is a basic contract between owners. These types of owner contracts are usually referred to as shareholders' agreements, operating agreements and buy-sell agreements. In small privately owned companies they serve to promote harmony among ownership.

Regardless of your personal beliefs and confidence in colleagues it would be unwise to dismiss the possibility of future misunderstanding, hostility, or animosity. Indeed many experienced business people believe owner agreements should be drawn up before the first day of business.

A buy-sell arrangement may be drawing as a stand alone contract. This is typically the case with corporations organized for small businesses. On the other hand, the convention for limited liability companies is to insert a buy-sell provision into the Operating Agreement.

Either way, when carefully and thoughtfully drafted, there should be very little room for controversy should owners ever decide to part ways. As such, an agreement is essential to preserve a fruitful relationship even after business separation.

A pivotal provision in the agreement is a valuation clause. Invariably upon departure, whether voluntary or not, each owner will expect fair remuneration. The problem is every person's view of what constitutes a fair amount is usually different.

A variety of legitimate valuation questions may arise concerning various tangible and intangible assets held by a business. The most highly debatable values surround goodwill, customer lists, trademarks and copyrights, as well as hard assets including equipment and real estate. Without a prescribed valuation approach different methods could produce results that vary widely.

> *A buy-sell agreement minimizes controversy and infighting over legal issues.*

For the reasons indicated, it is extremely important to agree in advance on a specific valuation approach. Valuation methods in buy-sell agreements usually differ from value determinations performed for bank loan purposes. Business valuations for buy-sell purposes are typically determined by agreed fixed price, appraisal process or predetermined formula.

It behooves entrepreneurs to seek advice from their team of professional advisors before deciding on an appropriate valuation approach. The type of methodologies are numerous. A brief survey of the most basic methods are as follows:

Net Book Value—Value is derived from equity reported on the balance sheet of the business.

Fair Market Value—Appraised value of net assets ordinarily set by outside appraisal or other professional assessor.

Formula—Prescribed formulas use average current and past net earnings adjusted for good will and any other intangibles.

After deciding the valuation approach principal owners give careful consideration to how the buyout provision in their agreement will actually be funded. Buy-sells are sometimes funded through life insurance in case of death or outright cash purchase in other situations. Alternatively, a payment plan in the form of a promissory note may be used. The latter could avoid the necessity for the remaining business owners to sell off operating assets just to generate the dollars to purchase the withdrawing owner's interest.

> *Most buy-sell arrangements are funded with life insurance.*

THE SILVER LINING

In the end, the silver lining beneath the marketing façade of most long standing businesses, is a tightly knitted business structure. Lack of legal structure need not be a weakness among many entrepreneurial companies. To the contrary, it should be a strength.

A solid legal structure should help improve policies and methods of management. For example, greater cohesion may result when the respective rights, privileges and duties of owners are spelled out in writing. Likewise certain internal guidelines as well as Bylaws, Operating and Shareholder's Agreements receive fine tuning.

Some of the more fundamental privileges, duties and rights that should be addressed as part of the process include the following:

- Voting Terms and Conditions
- Officer Designations and Responsibilities
- Stock Transfer Restrictions Rights, if any
- Admission to Ownership
- Compensation of Owners, if any
- Life Insurance on Key Officers
- Term of Business (i.e., Limited or Perpetual)

Other basic areas of legal governance and administration that also may be required include:

- Annual Meetings
- Special Meetings
- Place of Meetings
- Notice of Meetings
- Quorum
- Conduct and Location of Meetings

When owners regularly revisit these pivotal areas the risk of business break up over trivial issues of personality and discretion is much lower.

Finally, in some instances state statutes and regulations will dictate certain corporate governance rules and practices. Notable areas subject to variation in different jurisdictions include:

	CORPORATIONS	LLCs
MANAGEMENT ROLES AND RESPONSIBILITIES	The board of directors appoints officers to be responsible for management of specific divisions, including President/CEO (Chief Executive Officer); Vice President/COO (Chief Operating Officer); Controller/CFO (Chief Financial Officer). The board also designates the scope of specific duties and responsibilities for each officer in the bylaws. This structure provides a ready chain of command. The Board of Directors is elected by the owner/shareholders of the corporation	Owners, referred to as "Members," may elect to manage the affairs of the business collectively, appoint a member designated as the Manager, hire a non-member Manager, or create a structure with officers inclusive of President/CEO (Chief Operating Officer), and other officer positions.
DISTRIBUTION OF PROFITS AND LOSES	Ordinarily dividends have to be authorized by a majority of the board of directors or shareholders. Dividends normally are paid based on the number and class of stock shares held. Shareholders also can be compensated as employees for services rendered.	LLCs generally have discretion to decide how profits and losses will be allocated among members subject to special tax law regulations. Tiers of profit distribution may be agreed upon by the members. Members also may agree to make guaranteed payments as compensation to members for services rendered.

	CORPORATIONS	LLCs
CAPITAL INVESTMENT	Depending on jurisdiction eligible Close Corporations with a shareholder agreement can determine the maximum capital investment of shareholders. Otherwise corporate law in the jurisdiction controls rights over purchase of new stock shares.	By agreement members usually are allowed to specify minimum or maximum capital investment amounts; or provide voting discretion by majority to decide whether to invest additional capital. Most states permit the Operating Agreement to state applicable criteria.
ADMISSION OF NEW OWNER	Generally there is no limit on the number of shareholders unless otherwise stated in a governing document such as a Shareholder's Agreement. Majority of board or shareholders approve new stock issues. This is an ideal model for businesses with numerous investors or that plan to raise capital publicly as in an initial public offering (IPO).	Members generally are allowed to establish and/or vote on criteria for admission of a new member. Otherwise, consistent with laws of the jurisdiction the Operating Agreement usually establishes a maximum limit on the number of people who may become members.

NOTABLE REFLECTIONS AT A GLANCE

→ Limited legal liability protection is essential.

→ Strategic business planning entails management of legal risks.

→ Formal strategic relationships should be sufficiently documented.

→ Buy-sell agreements provide financial guidance in the event of withdrawal, death or disability.

→ Formalities in legal structure serve to preserve harmony among owners.

CHAPTER TEN
Guard the Upside...
Downsize Business Risks

| *The Journey* |

After agreeing on a legal structure, the business associates turned to carefully evaluate the worst case. BJ reminded Taylor how businesses took a nose-dive due to unexpected personal tragedies affecting the principals and that businesses often plummet after being victimized by a disaster.

Taylor suggested a visit to a financial professional for coverage in the event of death or disability of either party. She also suggested devising a disaster recovery plan.

BJ also recommended drawing up a succession strategy or plan to sell the business in the future. In the event they did not identify someone to take over such as a family member he wanted to be in position to put the business on the market at any time.

Taylor liked the concept of succession but felt increasing the value of their investment should be their first priority. In the end, she too wished for a large capital gain down the road.

Finally, BJ put on the table the possibility of forming of an advisory board or board of directors to help govern the new venture. He credits much of Matrix's success to the advice he received from his board. He believes the new venture could be well served by following the same practice.

Finally, your business is in full swing with steady sales growth, increasing profits, positive cash flow, and ample financing. Your dreams are coming true and you are flying high. Are you home free? Probably not.

Unless you have taken steps to manage risks, your company may be highly vulnerable to collapse. Most business veterans agree, the question is not whether or not a business owner will confront a potentially devastating occurrence but whether they have built a war chest to withstand the shock?

After working tirelessly to build a financially viable business, risking loss of your investment would be foolish. Yet, this often occurs when a business owner fails to actively manage risks. Even when they do, there still may be no way to completely downsize business risks.

If you are like most entrepreneurs your worst fears could be any one of the following...

- Your right hand person—the only employee trained to function at a management level—suddenly and unexpectedly resigns.

- Due to your own illness you are forced to take a leave of absence for several months or more.

- A major customer constituting a sizable portion of your business revenues files bankruptcy.

• Your hand picked successor is unable to continue their duties due to disability.

Under the buy-sell agreement a departing owner is entitled to a payment of $300,000, however, cash in the bank and from other sources only approximates $100,000.

Your principle business office is hit by a hurricane destroying vital business information such as customer sales, accounts receivable and disabling computer systems.

Entrepreneurs are confronted with these and other high risk concerns everyday. In this chapter my focus will be helping a business not only survive inherent threats but recover to good standing.

CHAPTER HIGHLIGHTS:

→ Income Protection

→ Back Up Resources

→ Maintaining Business Value

→ People Support Systems

→ Exit Strategies

→ Damage Control

BASIC LIFE SUPPORT

It would be naïve, and some might argue irresponsible to ignore risks associated with every day life. Most people believe in wisely taking steps to minimize the fall out if the worst happens. Because of their importance to maintaining the organization, loss of a business owner, CEO or key officer would be magnified two-fold. In fact, any major personal set back stands to have a major domino effect not only on their family but their company's employees and investors.

A study of the technical facets of insurance is far beyond the confines of this book. Suffice it to say, it is wise to consider carrying insurance against risks that could inflict serious and disastrous financial loss. Probably first among these concerns is health insurance. In most cases, health coverage is critical to provide company wide for various reasons. A healthy work force is a more productive team with lower absenteeism, keener focus and better overall performance.

It is well known that a substantial number of home foreclosures are tied to personal injuries and or sickness that result in discontinuation of employment. For working people as well as business owners, insurance coverage for disability, life and other critical areas is indispensable. The following is just a short list of the type of insurance protections that should be seriously considered by virtually anyone in business along with key personnel:

DISABILITY

Disability is a primary cause for default and foreclosure. This statement pertains to business loans as much as to residential mortgages. While some form of disability insurance coverage is highly advisable, a lack of coverage for disability is a common problem for business owners.

Disability insurance replaces lost wages when the insured is unable to work after a specific period of time. Most business owners are dependent on income from their businesses to maintain their households, and adequate coverage can insure their personal financial stability. In addition, disability coverage will avoid the potential depletion of the firm's cash by the owner in an attempt to support the owner's financial needs.

Typically, disability plans cover 60% to 70% of pre-tax earnings ninety days after becoming disabled. Your insurance professional can advise you on other important features regulating policy renewal and cancellation, inflation protection, rehabilitation assistance, and waiting periods.

LONG-TERM CARE

Long-term care is not a first thought for most people, let alone entrepreneurs and business owners. Coverage provides reimbursement for long-term care, including nursing stays and home care services. Premiums for long-term care insurance vary depending on age, deductible period, years of coverage, inflation protection and other options. Regardless of age prudent financial planning requires consideration of long-term care.

Most people cannot afford to pay for long-term care costs in the event of a catastrophic or prolonged illness. Skyrocketing health costs could financially wipe out the average person. Medicaid is not the answer if you have built sizable equity in your business and acquired other significant personal assets. To qualify for Medicaid under current regulations an individual first would have spend down his or her personal fortune. Long-term care insurance could prevent this eventuality while preserving your financial asset base.

LOSS OF LIFE

The key life insurance decision for business owners is determining the amount of necessary coverage. From a business perspective, the appropriate level of coverage depends on whether the policy is designed to fund buyout or provide recovery money for the business. The distinction can make a huge difference in selecting the amount of coverage. Moreover, life insurance can be an effective substitute and replacement for building cash reserves needed to fulfill personal and business commitments in the event of an entrepreneurs' death.

It also is common for companies to take out life insurance to protect the business against death of a key employee. You also may elect to carry life insurance to satisfy ownership buy-sell agreements. If not, the company may lack the financial means to pay the stipulated amount or valuation.

Deciding precisely how much coverage is an appropriate question to work through and is a matter that should be in consultation with your insurance and other professional advisors. Naturally, this decision usually varies on an individual basis. In any case, the goal should be to align an insurance protection to accommodate and provide a cushion to you and your family in the event a life changing circumstance does in fact occur.

SURVIVAL MONEY

In many cases, business failures can be traced to unforeseen economic or financial mishaps. Adverse developments at some time or another are inevitable in business life. Survival may depend on adequate back up funds to weather the storm. An absence of cash reserves will leave a company and its principal owners highly vulnerable.

If you operate a business one of the first things you will discover is that back-up capital is synonymous with emergency capital. Your rainy day stash not only covers operations for a reasonable period but both personal and business emergencies.

Personal financial planners commonly recommend maintaining at lease three months costs of living. There is obviously a reasonable justification for this yardstick based on the daily challenges people face in our society. With the ever increasing number and frequency of corporate consolidations or reorganizations the probability of a layoff or transition in employment is relatively high. Accordingly, financial planners aim to ready their clients by creating a set aside of funds.

Just like a working person, the personal income of business owners may be adversely affected by factors outside their control. These circumstances may arise due to non-renewal of a commercial line of credit, bankruptcy of a major customer, change of laws, loss of a key employee or a business downturn. If they do not have back up funds these types of events could ruin them financially.

By comparison to an employed individual, a business owner has many people's livelihoods at stake. A savings or investment reserve of two months operating expenses, may not be the appropriate savings level. More likely, their personal emergency money may need to be raised by a percent of their company's minimum working capital. Estimating a reasonable back fund for a business owner is far dicier than for the average individual.

For entrepreneurs launching a start-up, the threshold may be even greater because of the initial risks. During ramp up of a new venture, sales forecasts and expense budgets may vary significantly from the forecast. Likewise, cash collections from customer sales may lag much longer than expected. Generally, revenue and expense patterns tend to be highly volatile. In addition, operators usually confront a steep learning curve especially if they have no prior business experience.

On the other, even an established business is subject to the whims of a wide range of troublesome economic forces. For example, credit may tighten in the overall economy. In periods of tight credit and fear of business downturn banks and other financial institutions are less inclined to renew or extend credit even to some long standing customers. Because banks usually reserve the right to review a credit line periodically and decide whether to cancel, it always makes sense to have a back up fund. Recent history indicates sole reliance on bank credit as a lifeline can be a mistake.

> *Even with a well-conceived business plan, actual performance may vary drastically from forecasts*

In general, business owners should err on the side of maintaining excess backup funds. Even with a well-conceived business plan, actual performance may vary drastically from forecast.

Volatility in revenues and expenses is also inherently greater in some businesses than others. In the final analysis, it is a wise practice to prepare for the worst since the best case will take care of itself.

ASSET MAINTENANCE

Unlike residential real estate there are no well publicized listings to pinpoint the going values of different businesses. Even if you found one it would not necessarily be indicative of price for a particular company because so many subjective as well as objective factors come into play.

As a private business a significant amount of your personal wealth may be tied up in the business. It behooves anyone in this position to take every feasible measure to boost the value of the investment using all reasonable means.

A complete discussion of the many technical and judgmental approaches for business valuation is beyond the focus of this book. Nevertheless, a brief discussion of the rudiments of business valuation as it impacts a business owner and other principal investors is called for.

In the actual sale of a business a variety of tangible and intangible qualities are typically valued. While certain assets may be assessed as a group, others are separated and appraised on an individual basis. On the other hand, buyers are sometimes only interested in purchasing certain assets rather than the company as a whole.

The projected future income of a business may be the dominant pricing ingredient. Ordinarily, these types of pricing projections are discounted using present interest rates. On the contrary, in certain industries a multiple of gross sales over several recent years is the standard rule of thumb. In this situation business values really depend on revenue generating capacity.

In light of these variations, valuation should be managed like any other major investment in your personal portfolio. It pays to regularly assess your portfolio. Many items may be intangible. Goodwill is one possibility. Goodwill may be tied up in customer contracts, long standing reputation, operating systems, technical training and expertise. While these items typically do not get reported on the balance sheet or income statement they could be a critical element for business valuation and sale purposes.

Likewise, companies sometimes possess precious intellectual property by way of customized software, patents, copyrights and licenses. It is not only essential to obtain these rights in the first instance, but to comply with applicable regulations to maintain the legal integrity of such assets. For all types of assets proof of legal title and ownership is also vital. In the end, you must be able to validate your rights and legal authority to make an asset transfer.

In some cases, a record of repairs and maintenance on major office and operating equipment will serve to booster value. Also, possessing legal authority to transfer manufacture warranties and other protections could carry notable worth. The more you know and understand the worth of every asset in your business portfolio, the more proactive you can be to ensure that each business asset continues to hold its value.

For instance, personnel records and employment contracts could be valuable for a service enterprise where specialized labor is key. With continued protection the buyer may have less fear about a mass exodus after the business is exchanged. That discomfort may make them inclined to insist on discounting the price.

Finally, the quality of your financial statements and tax returns will invariably carry added significance. Buyers usually place a great deal of reliance on them to support their suppositions regarding a business. To the extent they lack consistency or reliability this will tend to bring down business value.

It is safe to assume some of the variables discussed will be pivotal to the sales price of virtually every business. The future sales price of a business could be impacted negatively or positively based on current decisions of management. To maximize future value it is wise to study established practices of business valuation for your industry.

EXIT STRATEGIES

Seasoned business veterans agree, in order to launch a successful business you need an overarching business strategy covering entry, operations and exit. Unfortunately, far too often the exit plan is put on the backburner or completely ignored until the business owner is in a pinch.

Exit planning is critical in case sale or transfer of a privately owned company is necessitated by illness, disability or premature death. Under these circumstances are well formulated, an exit strategy will be invaluable. Most private business owners either transfer by succession or outright sale.

Transfer by succession may be accomplished simply by grooming a family member or an insider to take over the business. Assuming the desired outcome, the person or persons under consideration for succession will probably need time to be properly trained and educated on the inner workings of business. Specialized management and industry training may be necessary as well as along with special job experience. A succession process is normally sequenced and coordinated to build talent and capabilities of the chosen successor. Otherwise, the person may be unprepared and squash the vitality of the business.

Even when the success process is tightly managed there is no certainty the plan will come to fruition. The heir apparent may leave the employ of the company or simply later decline the invitation to take on ownership. On the other hand, as principal owner you could have a change of heart about their suitability for business ownership. Any of these developments could throw a succession plan off track. Therefore, a strategy for outright business sale should never be summarily discarded.

An exit strategy based on business sale must be flexible. It should provide several possible avenues for business exchange. For example, a business owner might consider selling ownership to others in increments by doling out a portion of stock to them over a specific time interval, say every five years if they continue to work for the business. Public companies are widely known to use a version of this approach with a grant of restricted employee stock option plans. The approach creates an incentive for the best people to stay and also gives them a stake in the outcome of business operations.

> *Business transition and succession planning should begin on the very first day of operations.*

A plan to exit by selling the business in the future may necessitate identifying potential buyers far in advance. Also, special types of business marketing may play a key role. There are of course business brokers and investment bankers who offer this type of assistance.

On the other hand, a business owner may consider taking their company "public," by offering ownership interest to the general public. This strategy would amount to cashing out by converting private to public ownership. The requisite time and effort to make all the necessary arrangements may be a factor in deciding direction. Nevertheless, this alternative could be the most lucrative way to cash out.

Many aspects of exit planning and preparation are commonsense. Think for a moment about the steps most people take to avoid losing money on a home purchase. When choosing residential property most will evaluate their family needs and lifestyle. However, perhaps more important is how salable the property will be in the future. In essence, most people evaluate resale proposition even before they buy.

Homebuyers and entrepreneurs share the same economic objective as it relates to resale. In the case of entrepreneurs, they have to also assess the prospects of resale and make prudent upgrades to assure future resale. Just like homeowners business owners have to take care to make improvements and renovations to their property.

When it comes to enhancing a business investment, entrepreneurs should operate with the mentality that regular service and maintenance is incumbent. Moreover, it is essential to wisely invest in operations, infrastructure, systems and personnel development in order to stand to reap maximum gain in the future. In fact, exit preparation and planning should begin on day one.

Good Samaritans

Even the most enlightened entrepreneur is less likely to succeed without help from of others. In order to sustain upward momentum over the long-term, entrepreneurs usually rely on a nucleus of close advisors. These people consist of mentors, family and friends; your support system also consists of seasoned business minds.

With so many complex and strategic decisions on the table to make, people in business can easily lose focus, overlook opportunity or simply fatigue. With the constant pressure of critical decision making, entrepreneurs and CEOs need for a support base becomes critical.

Most large public companies setup a "kitchen cabinet" in the form of a board of directors charged with management oversight and helping to navigate uncharted waters. Such boards provide experience and insight that can be extremely valuable for strategic planning purposes as well. This support base sometimes offers more objectivity because insiders may be beholden to top management and less inclined to offer candid feedback.

Without the benefit of a kitchen cabinet, CEOs and managers tend to become wedded to one school of thought, thereby losing the advantage of another perspective. Regardless of size, no business can afford to be myopic in its approach in the marketplace. Accordingly, large and small businesses alike need a kitchen cabinet to assure progress and competitiveness. Should your thinking falter or stray off track, the board is in position to redirect the thought process.

Some may think it is very complicated to formalize a board. However, the two popular models are relatively straight forward. Most businesses have the option of creating a board of directors or board of advisors. A formal board of directors must normally be legally approved by the shareholders or members of the company. Furthermore, it is worth noting that under the laws of most states, the decisions and resolutions of a board of directors are legally binding on management. By contrast, recommendations and advice of a board of advisors generally are nonbinding.

Many investors and lenders consider the board a very important component of the management infrastructure. In fact, highlighting the educational and business backgrounds of board members in a business plan generally adds value to the plan. Those who have served as advisors for successful companies in the past will certainly carry significant weight.

Just like for large public companies, for privately owned businesses an outside leadership group can help map strategy to circumvent a bad outcome.

Just like for large public companies, an outside leadership group can help map strategy to circumvent a bad outcome for privately owned businesses also.

In addition to pure guidance, members of the board are often a handy source of leads for new customers and investors. People intricately acquainted with the business model and operations also can be effective advocates for entrepreneurs in the early stages of development.

Boards are also a viable avenue for gaining access to specialized talent and expertise; such as, engineering, architecture, computer science and other specialized fields. Likewise, persons with extensive business experience may be willing to support the business through participation on a board. Oddly, it might be desirable to have someone on your board who previously failed in business. Their knowledge and experience could be invaluable essentially for the lessons learned.

Finally, another highly instrumental part of a company's support base is its team of professional advisors – lawyers, accountants, insurance advisors, real estate brokers, financial planners, etc. It is best in most cases to solicit their input and assistance prior to undertaking any major business decision. In fact, this approach is far less costly than seeking their advice for correcting mistakes on the back end.

Damage Control

In recent times, disaster preparation has become a high priority for a growing number of companies. Virtually every business regardless of size stands to be destroyed by a natural or human engineered disaster. In order to recover financially, adequate contingent preparations are essential. At a minimum, every company should develop a set of disaster plans. In so doing, the list of questions below could help to direct the focus:

- What type of catastrophic events are you most vulnerable to operationally, managerially and administratively?

- How probable are these unfortunate events likely to occur?

- In the worst case, what would be the financial, legal and operational costs?

- Are company personnel set to manage a recovery process or will this require outside contractors and/or be dependent on public emergency assistance?

- If the company officer, contractor or outside party with primary responsibility for crisis management is unavailable, who else will be tapped to act as a surrogate to direct emergency response?

Your company's level of disaster readiness could determine whether it survives or falters after a tragedy. Commonly referred to as "Acts of God" in contracts, events such as tornado, hurricane, or severe weather storm could be crippling. There are also so called "man made" incidents of crisis that can

Your company's level of disaster readiness could determine whether it survives or falters after a tragedy.

have a terrible impact. Needless to say, most of these risks cannot be eliminated. However, prudent measures can be taken to relieve the extent of damage.

Fortunately, in most jurisdictions local, State and Federal authorities have paved the way with documented programs and best practices for emergency response. Public resource guides covering channels of information dissemination and emergency response protocols are now widely available. For most companies this means they only need to craft limited contingency plans that feed into public resources.

On an individual basis emergency plans and preparations may vary based on company size, geographic location, technological resources and many other factors. Nevertheless, disaster plans will normally share some common fundamental elements as listed on the next page:

Naturally, to ensure that an emergency response plan is fully operational periodic tests similar to a routine fire drill should be planned. Each year some organizations use crisis specific conditions for this purpose in what are called "table top" exercises. Every three years they may engage in a full blown emergency response practice. This work is essential to maintain readiness. In today's world, emergency preparation is absolutely indispensable.

DISASTER PLANNING OUTLINE

Employee Information

- Contact Information
- Phone Tree
- Transportation Alternatives
- Emergency Housing Options
- Financial Needs
- Childcare Availability
- Disaster Pay and Overtime Policies

Key Contacts

- Customers
- Banks
- Partners and Investors
- Insurance Agents
- Accountants
- Lawyers
- Utilities
- Police, Fire and Rescue

Suppliers and Vendors

- Contact Information
- Geographic Diversity
- Back-Up Sources
- Credit Arrangements

Business Functions

- Most Critical
- Allowable Downtime
- Legal Obligations to Customers, Creditors
- Recovery Locations
- Internal Communications Plans
- External Communications Plans
- Computer Networks and Back-Up
- Software Programs
- Inventory
- Equipment
- Vehicles
- Utilities
- Payroll
- Regulatory Requirements
- Accounts Payable
- Accounts Receivable

Preparatory Measures

- Written Policies
- Operations Manual
- Training
- Simulations

NOTABLE REFLECTIONS AT A GLANCE

→ The essential forms of the life support for business owners include health, disability, life and long-term care.

→ The standard level of cash back-up for emergencies is higher for entrepreneurs.

→ Maximizing business value requires maintaining and growing the worth of significant business assets.

→ Exit strategies and planning should begin prior to opening operations.

→ Boards of Advisors and Directors serve to strengthen strategic planning and preparation.

→ Disaster planning is critical to minimize the risk of devastation.

CHAPTER ELEVEN
Gradually Stockpile Reserves...
Earmark Strategic Priorities

| *The Journey* |

Losing money is not BJ's biggest fear. Instead, he is most fearful the company will not be positioned to secure financial backing for growth. He envisions competing in the global marketplace in the not too distant future, but realizes it will be very difficult to finance expansion through conventional bank financing. Instead, from the very start BJ would like to put aside a percentage of profits earned and use this as seed money to explore new markets, enlarge capacity and develop new products.

On the other hand, Taylor's main goal is current income. She believes aggressive growth will not allow for ample amount of distributions to the owners. In fact, she wants to form an agreement on specific guidelines for when and how much profit will be made available for distribution to owners on an annual basis. She also wants the partners to agree on their regular compensation levels.

Finally, prior to setting a launch date for the joint venture, BJ recommends engaging a tax professional to evaluate the basic income tax ramifications of their plans. Although the partners expect the business will incur operating losses for the first two years, they believe it will generate substantial profits thereafter.

Lack of reserves to underwrite the cost of implementation is one of the main reasons so many promising business plans lay dormant. If you don't earmark funds necessary to turn plans into action, it usually proves to be a fruitless exercise. Typically, entrepreneurs stop the strategic process short of considering effective ways to free up dollars to move the company to the next level. Raising funds from outside sources is not always a plausible solution.

Most companies begin their long-term strategic planning by identifying and determining how much profit is possible to earmark to meet strategic priorities. The next critical step is determining a plausible source of funding. If you don't consider these issues early on you may find your company constantly in a state of flux financially and unable to move ahead strategically.

The aim of this chapter is to introduce an array of fundamental priorities that warrant long-term strategic planning and budgeting.

CHAPTER HIGHLIGHTS:

✦ Strategic Funding

✦ Designated Reserves

✦ Distributions to Owners

✦ Debt Management and Retirement

✦ Provisions for Income Taxes

SEED MONEY

Virtually every business has a need to amass seed money to pursue future business opportunities. Seed money is of course necessary to defray the cost of attracting new customers and retaining old ones. Seed money is also key to developing new lines of products and services.

Naturally, resources for marketing research, product testing, expert consulting, education and training precede the roll out of a new line of products or services. Funding makes it possible to explore new markets and product development opportunities. Ideally seed money should be an integral part of the operating budget.

Seed funding is predicated on a portion of business profits being designated for business development. Even though activities undertaken may not always generate returns immediately such investments are key to long-term business survival and prosperity. To implement the practice takes fiscal discipline to fight off the temptation to use these resources for other immediate purposes.

There are no hard and fast rules on how to create a set aside for seed money. However, it stands to reason most companies should begin with itemizing prospective needs, quantifying financial resources, and setting a time line for achieving the savings objective.

A shining example of a company that has long realized that a profitable future was tied to investing in the next generation of products and services is Microsoft. The company's strategic push was probably best described in a Wall Street Journal article entitled, "Behind Microsoft's Bid to Gain Cutting Edge."

> When Bill Gates announced his plan to retire, Craig Mundie was appointed the company's chief research and strategy thinker.

As reported in the Wall Street Journal, "The challenge, he says, is anticipating what new technologies have the potential to become a big business for the company, or conversely, to threaten its foundation."

Microsoft maintains research facilities all over the globe, and Mr. Mundie travels an estimated 200,000 miles per year meeting with researchers and customers. He identifies potentially viable technologies, and coordinates development of compatible products in various parts of the world.

The firm invests in immature technologies considered promising and helps develop them into commercially viable products. The company also purchases potentially competitive and innovative firms to acquire their technologies. Finally, Microsoft often uses small groups of experts from a variety of functions to develop and test specialized products.

As Mr. Mundie described it, "You've got to have a small number of people who think that it's their job to take risks ... I view my job, in part, as making sure that the company supports the things that take time but end up being big."[1]

Although the scale of Microsoft's drive to develop new business opportunities may be considerably more ambitious than the average entrepreneur, the Company's resolve to stay competitive and profitable in the industry offers a valuable lesson that is universally applicable. Rather than rest on your laurels during profitable periods, it is important to discipline your business to stay in the hunt. Entrepreneurial companies especially can least afford to sit back passively and expect to hold on to their market share.

The world's population is estimated to increase by approximately 2 billion people, to 8 billion by 2020. According to the National Research Council of Canada (NCRC), the bulk of the growth will occur in developing countries such as China, India and Indonesia. Increased globalization should impact the rate of population expansion throughout the world. "Asian culture will profoundly shape global interactions, societal values and behaviors."[2]

These emerging markets will provide a wealth of new growth opportunities for domestic firms. The positive benefits are already

> *The global economy will be impacted by population growth in developing countries such as China, India and Indonesia*

being felt in many sectors. *The Wall Street Journal* reported:

> *Charles Reinhard, director of portfolio strategy at asset-management firm Neuberger Berman, estimates that companies in the S&P 500 derive about 30% of their revenue from abroad, up from 22% five years ago. U.S. companies also get a big chuck of profits from overseas operations: According to data from the Commerce Department, foreign subsidiaries accounted for about 24% of U.S. after-tax corporate profits in 2006, compared with 17% a decade ago. (The number does not include exports from the U.S.)[3]*

Another significant trend at the opening of the 21st century is the aging of our population and the associated dramatic growth in health care industries. Experts predict the number of people aged 65 and older will exceed the number of children aged 15 and under by mid-century.[4]

As the global marketplace evolves many believe entrepreneurial businesses stand to benefit the most. Technological advances, the internet and advent of virtual offices provide a convenient step ladder for small agile companies to serve a world market. Technology truly becomes the great equalizer. However, seed money will no doubt serve to position the average business to seize these emerging opportunities.

BUSINESS REINVESTMENT DOLLARS

Reinvesting dollars back into a company is analogous to regular automobile service and maintenance. For a vehicle to hold up over time and operate at peak level, the engine and other key operating parts must be serviced and refurbished on a routine basis. In business the key objective of a maintenance program is to extend its productive life cycle.

Companies that own and manage real estate often keep a reserve for replacements in connection with roofing, paving as well as heating and ventilation. They understand the virtue of saving ahead of time to replace key components of a commercial building, operating equipment and parts. Companies in virtually every industry should consider adopting some form of this approach in connection with major cost items they know will eventually require replacement.

For instance, most service enterprises are on schedule to dispose of, expand or replace their operating infrastructure. As a practical matter, this could pertain to computer systems, software, communication devices, transportation equipment, training aids and other items of an essential nature. From a funding perspective, it would be unwise to delay amassing internal resources and solely rely on outside funding especially if the business is generating positive returns. Saving incrementally could normalize the impact and minimize future financing requirements.

Unlike capital intensive businesses, service enterprises are not inclined to make adequate provisions for future replacements. The overwhelming numbers of these businesses are at risk for reason of merely living in the here and now. On the other hand, those with a proactive management agenda make it a key mission to establish a reserve fund to offset costs of new infrastructure. At the rate of new technology this is no doubt a very wise business practice.

For the reasons cited there is every reason to establish a reserve for replacements. The key is to take action long before visible signs of financial deterioration set in. In other words, the company's prompting in this area need not wait until there is a history of chronic equipment failures, low employee morale, loss of customers or a string of financial losses. These types of symptoms are sometimes irreversible.

The budget parameters of course should be business specific. The focus should be on replacements anticipated over the next two to five years. The review process may spill over into business planning because of the correlation to operational expectations. A blueprint of how business will function in the future has to be part of the thought process.

Long range business plans must be defined to ascertain the funding needs and requirements of a replacement reserve.

Developing reliable replacement cost estimates is also an integral part of the replacement reserve planning. Best results are predicated on current prices adjusted for inflation. Using applicable indexes like the consumer price index a forecast of the cost and future funding is not difficult for most companies. Economic realities should be built into the model. At worst case, even if the forecasts prove inaccurate at least the business will have succeeded in setting aside a funding base.

Funding replacement reserves on a monthly basis should be the goal. In the long term the savings schedule should correspond to expected obsolescence. The overriding objective is to implement a savings plan that will position the business financially to underwrite all or a significant portion of the replacement costs in the future.

POP-UP COSTS

A mistake capable of quickly derailing a sound financial plan is failure to budget what I refer to as "pop up costs". These are financial obligations that will sprout up at a certain time in the future. They range from planned office relocations to legal settlements. For the most part they are big ticket items.

The overriding danger is that a major cost will pop-up at a time when operating cash is at its lowest level. Under these circumstances a business could find itself in serious financial jeopardy. A wise approach would be to gradually build a reserve to cover these types of obligations rather than run the risk of confronting an unfunded obligation that requires draconian measures.

> *The overriding danger is that a pop-up will surface at a time when operating cash is at its lowest level.*

For instance, quite often operating equipment under lease provides for a buy-out option at the end. This is classic type of pop up item that begs for advance funding. If the option price is significant payment may exact an unmanageable drain on cash flow.

The spectrum of special funding requirements for non-routine purposes can be quite extensive. Arguably, balloon payments on commercial business loans as well as investor buyout agreements should be considered. In addition, any high deductible commercial property and casualty insurance policies may be taken into account because a substantial deductible would have to be borne by the company.

Certain types of future financial commitments may not be precisely quantifiable. For example, when companies sell or factor their accounts receivables the potential reverse payout may not be readily known. Generally, if certain customers fail to make payment within a specific period of time the business will be subject to charge-backs. Probably the most effective way for these companies to operate is to maintain a charge back reserve based on historical experience.

Similarly, it is sometimes difficult to gauge the appropriate reserve requirements for businesses that extend product and service warranties. To prevent becoming overexposed financially they too should find it beneficial to establish a reserve to defray the estimated costs of labor and materials associated with product and service warranties.

In a select number of industries it is advisable to create general contingency funds for unspecified purposes because of a normal persistent flux in business activity. For example, general and government contracting businesses routinely experience lags between the beginning of new contracts and completion of old ones. Without a set aside to fund ongoing expenses contractors may be forced to downsize, cut their regular labor force and sell off operating assets to survive. Many seasonal businesses confront the same type of challenges and depend on off season reserves.

The first step toward providing adequate coverage is completing an inventory of the various pop up obligations on the horizon. In turn, this will allow financial preparation based on expected future obligations. The next step is of course to begin to set aside financial resources systematically.

Another source of information about contingent obligations is certified financial statements. Under Generally Accepted Accounting

Principles, footnote disclosures should provide information about known fixed future financial obligations. This includes long term leases, commercial loans, pending lawsuits and other matters that may materially impact the business.

> *The first step toward building a reserve is to complete an inventory of the various pop-up obligations on the horizon.*

In addition to surveying financial statements, a thorough review of major legal agreements should be considered. They may contain provisions that have financial significance or reveal the probability of additional financial exposure.

In essence, the driving force behind appropriating funds for special future needs is to avoid being blind sided. You should always strive to maintain coverage for pop-ups that could have a major financial impact.

JACKPOT FOR INVESTORS

Returns to investors are usually measured in two basic ways, dividends received and appreciation in investment. Unfortunately, private businesses do not trade their stock on a national exchange market, therefore demonstrating real increases in the market value of shareholder investments is not easy to show.

Just because earnings and profits are reflected in the financial statements, does not necessarily mean the value of an investment has not increased nor that liquid expendable funds are readily available to pay dividends to principal owners and investors. Only in very rare cases will the retained earnings reported in the balance sheet fully tell the story.

For most companies the lion's share of retained earnings (often labeled members' capital for a limited liability company, owners' equity for a sole proprietorship) is tied up in accounts receivables and operating assets such as machinery equipment and buildings. Therefore, when evaluating investor payouts, you must look beyond reported retained earnings towards real liquidity, namely, cash. Rarely will a business owner have the luxury to drain earnings and profits reflected as part of retained earnings on the balance sheet.

In terms of affordability, distributable earnings have to be carefully evaluated. Typically, you begin with a liquidity assessment and then review strategic priorities.

The dilemma for entrepreneurs and corporate decision makers is appeasing investors while not sacrificing too much. They wrestle with balancing the desire to handsomely reward their investors and their responsibility to keep the business positioned to continue to fund ongoing needs. These two overriding objectives are sometimes difficult to mesh.

Retained earnings reported in the balance Sheet may not represent cash in liquid form.

In public companies, a powerful board of directors is empowered to set dividend policy and make the final call on such matters. They too weigh investor expectations against fundamental business needs and requirements. On the other hand, the founder or controlling principals in entrepreneurial businesses must decide timing, manner and approach to use in rewarding investors.

Needless to say whether your business is publicly or privately owned sound business judgment is paramount when it comes to directing the use of resources. To maintain the weight of decision making power it pays not to give up a majority of voting control.

From the perspective of your investors it is probably wise to weigh possible income tax ramifications of any planned distribution. Corporations, for example, ordinarily account for income taxes at the business level rather than pass them along to its individual shareholders. However, when a regular corporation pays out dividends to its shareholders they too must pay income taxes on these dollars. This bunching of income taxes is commonly referred to as "double taxation."

> *In public companies a powerful board of directors determines if, when and how much dividends to pay out.*

Fortunately, the law provides that relatively small private corporations may opt out of a structure at risk for double taxation. There are a rigid set of standards to be classified as a Subchapter S for income tax purposes. A key potential advantage is a corporation just like LLCs, partnerships and sole proprietorships will only act as a "pass through entity." Rather than the business itself being responsible for the income taxes, the burden for reporting and paying income tax will fall on the individual shareholders.

Suffice it to say there can be many downsides to a Subchapter S election as well. Rarely, are any tax elections void of traps and possible negative consequences. This is the primary reason well informed business owners will not make a tax move without first enlisting the advice and guidance of a qualified tax professional.

In order to serve the best interests of investors, a comprehensive evaluation of the current and future income tax status of a business will probably be beneficial. Generally speaking, tax analysis should precede any definite decision about investor distributions.

INCOME TAX ALLOWANCE

If you operate a profitable business, liability for income taxes comes with the territory. For businesses and individuals prosperous enough to generate taxable income, their annual obligation, with certain exceptions, is required to be paid "as you go" in quarterly installments. The installments are tied to the annual estimated tax expense.

Of course it is smart to pay the aforementioned quarterly estimated tax deposits on a timely basis because it will avoid applicable penalties. However, perhaps even more important, cumulatively these deposits will reduce financial exposure for any unpaid income taxes at the end of the tax year. Without a cushion, many businesses would experience a profitable year but be at risk that their liability would exceed cash on deposit.

The litany of tax rules and regulations sometimes make it difficult to reliably estimate annual income tax expense and unfortunately, ignorance is not a defense. Therefore, entrepreneurs as well as CEOs have to exercise extreme care not to leave their businesses exposed and unprepared financially to meet any income tax obligations. The potential pitfalls and traps are far beyond the scope of this book. Only certain concepts surrounding income taxation will be highlighted.

For example, in preparing to derive an estimate of the annual amount of income taxes, one of the most challenging areas for small business owners and investors, especially those actually employed by the business, is taxable compensation. Compensation for services along with taxable income attributed to the earnings of the business can be a double whammy. Owners and investors who fall into taxation on both ends quickly discover that income tax accounting is far from straight forward.

In arriving at the bottom line number for income tax purposes, the timing and sometimes the amount of deductions vary from ways the same activity is reported on the financial statements. For instance, specific income tax regulations may dictate that deductibility depends on the timing of an expenditure (that is, depend on whether funds were spent in a specific tax year), income level (that is, eligibility for deductions may phase out at certain income thresholds) or vary according to type of legal entity (corporation, limited liability company, or sole proprietorship).

> *Tax deductions are typically contingent on timing (funds being spent in a specific time period), income level (benefits may be restricted or phased out with income) or type of legal entity (corporation, limited liability company, or sole proprietorship).*

DEBT RETIREMENT

The purpose of a debt sinking fund is to accumulate sufficient funds to retire major debt obligations such as mortgages, commercial term loans as well as investor buyouts. In the case of investor buyouts, the price and date to exercise a repurchase of stock may be stipulated in the same way a business loan sets a specific maturity date. In either case, a business has to be positioned financially to meet the terms as agreed.

Another compelling motivation for establishing a so called debt sinking fund is to accelerate repayment of debt ahead of schedule. The incentive behind the initiative could be to lessen the burden of regular monthly debt payments on cash flow. Also, the motive could be to improve the company's debt to equity ratio overall.

Furthermore, after a certain period of time the various restrictive covenants in the typical commercial loan agreement may become a hindrance to repositioning and business decision making. Loan covenants for example, may stipulate the maximum level of executive compensation, earnings available for distribution to owners, sale of certain business assets and other matters normally within management's discretion. At some junction these and other type of limitations may be considered an impediment.

On the other hand, a debt sinking fund may be a matter of necessity. Some commercial loans contain balloon or major principal payments that are legally required after a specific number of years. These loans may be structured with "a five year term and twenty year amortization." In this situation, lower monthly payment during the five year term of the loan would be followed by a substantial payoff at the end of the fifth year.

Insufficient cash to meet a balloon payment is simply not an option. It would risk foreclosure against business assets pledged as collateral and invoke any personal guarantees made by principal owners of a business. Based on the possible consequences a debt sinking fund would be advisable even if plan A calls for seeking refinancing of the business loan at maturity.

Naively, many business owners assume the option to refinance will always be available and opt not to build up a debt sinking fund. However, most seasoned veterans will agree promises of future refinancing is no security blanket. There is no guarantee your business will qualify for financing under the criteria in effect years into the future. Also, as recent history has shown the credit market is subject to sour at any time leaving you without a ready source of financing.

Generally speaking, debt has to be managed strategically to avoid becoming overleveraged. When this happens, a business will be under extreme pressure to maintain profits at current levels or risk default on their outstanding loans. Preferably, as discussed earlier in Chapter 7 it is best to maintain a healthy blend between debt and equity.

Eligibility for refinancing in the future should never be taken for granted.

Setting aside dollars to ease the path toward debt elimination is a strategy used by major companies especially when they become cash heavy during a robust business cycle. Quite often public companies negotiate for convertible debt, that is, debt that can be converted to equity in the form of stock. In entrepreneurial businesses, this avenue could also be considered for loans made to the company by principal owners and shareholders.

For all the good it provides at various times during a business' life cycle, most every company grows to desire more breathing room. Absent retiring debt per se, a debt management approach may be to search out the most economical opportunities to refinance at a lower interest rate. Debt capital is much like any other commodity; price should generally be the main determinant.

A wide range of variables may come into play when evaluating when to retire or refinance. Interest rate trends as well as any lines to investor capital are among the most common considerations. At the end of the day, managing business debt effectively will require as much thoughtful planning and analysis as your pricing and profit strategy overall.

The mechanics of setting up a debt sinking fund are relatively straight forward. Similar to any other designated savings a specific appropriation should be earmarked and budgeted from cash flow. It usually involves setting aside a specific dollar amount on a monthly or quarterly basis as a reserve fund that may be in the form of an investment or depository account.

SYNOPSIS OF PIVOTAL TAX MATTERS FOR BUSINESS ENTERPRISES AND THEIR OWNERS

Estimating taxable income can be a complex exercise. Many small business owners elect to report their business and personal income on their personal income tax return. In addition to the income taxes that arise just from these sources, business owners may also have to consider self-employment and alternative minimum taxes.

A bare bones chart designed to depict the interlocking effects of the tax structure for business owners and investors is illustrated below:

Sole Proprietorship

1. Taxable Income—Income tax plus subject to self employment tax.

2. Distributions to Owner– Non-taxable (previously reported taxable income).

Limited Liability Company/Partnership

1. Taxable Income—Taxable to members at their applicable individual marginal tax rates and subject to self employment tax.

2. Distribution to Members—Non-taxable (previously reported as taxable income).

3. Guaranteed Payments to Members (for services rendered)— Taxable to recipient at individual marginal rates.

Corporation

1. Taxable Income—Taxable at corporation's applicable marginal income tax rates.

2. Distributions to Shareholders (dividend)—Taxable to individual shareholder at individual rates.

3. Wages (for services rendered)—Taxable to receipt shareholder at individual marginal tax rates.

Subchapter S Corporation

1. Taxable Income—Taxable to individual shareholder at applicable individual marginal tax rates.

2. Distribution to Shareholders—Non-taxable (previously taxed).

3. Wages—Taxable to individual at applicable individual marginal tax rate.

As the outline suggests many facets of income tax law may cause your financial plan to go askew. Accordingly, to every extent possible you want to avoid overlooking any basic income tax provisions and factors. In addition, you most assuredly want to build these quarterly income tax deposits into your cash flow projection.

Hopefully, this discussion has succeeded in highlighting the breath of twists and turns that must be managed as they relate to income taxes. Perhaps even more important, was the goal to make you aware of the need to enlist the advice and counsel of a qualified tax professional. Otherwise, you could find yourself stuck in a big hole and caught in an endless game of catch up.

NOTABLE REFLECTIONS AT A GLANCE

→ Seed money designated for new market development warrants a reservation of funds.

→ Business reinvestment is essential to extend the business life cycle.

→ A reserve for debt management and retirement serves to reduce dependency and cost of debt financing.

→ Special funding should be set aside for anticipated major outlays of funds above and beyond normal operations.

→ Returns to investors should be stored in the form of cash or appreciated investment value.

→ Making quarterly income tax deposits reduces the extent of financial exposure at the end of the tax year.

CHAPTER TWELVE
Finish in the Black…
Champion Profitable Growth

| *The Journey* |

BJ and Taylor agree to an official launch date for their joint venture and turned their attention to growth projections. They agreed to strive to grow the company at an annual rate of twenty percent over the next three years. They also hope to squeeze out a profit by the end of the second year.

Taylor will concentrate on sales and marketing, while BJ's role will be mainly operations management. The team also agreed to form a board of advisors. Additionally, a meeting with legal counsel will be set to address legal structure.

Assuming their sales and operating objectives are achieved, BJ and Taylor will be able to qualify for private equity funding within three years. By year seven the company should be financially positioned to either take the company public or sell outright.

Athletes learn the basics of any sport before tackling sophisticated moves and strategies.

Drawing from the analogy of an athlete in training, the healthy development of a business not only lies with entrepreneurs who stand to benefit greatly from learning and practicing proven financial methods but strategies for achieving profitable growth.

Growth per se can be a two edge sword; it can propel a business to new and glorious heights financially or condemn it to ruin. The cliché that some businesses grow themselves out of business contains many grains of truth. If you don't learn to avoid pitfalls, growth can inflict business harm financially and operationally.

Profitable growth draws a clear distinction between good and bad growth. Simply put, good growth represents new business that contributes financially to the bottom line and offers an intangible benefit by way of goodwill, customer satisfaction, employee retention, and productivity.

Profitable growth is measured by a strong rate of new sales revenues matched by a robust climb in net income. In contrast, bad growth is counterproductive and takes a heavy toll on customer service, operating efficiency and financial stability. In the long term, the costs of bad growth far outweigh the benefits.

This chapter focuses on cultivating and managing healthy growth.

CHAPTER HIGHLIGHTS:

→ Balancing Growth and Profit

→ Parameters of Healthy Growth

→ Embracing Best Practices

→ Strategic Preparation and Execution

→ Capacity Building

THE BALANCING ACT

The most significant task confronting the CEO of virtually every business is maintaining profitable growth. A company that masters the art is bound for long-term success and financial prosperity.

I deferred discussion of profitable growth to the very end because without the benefit of a working knowledge of the pros and cons and the dos and don'ts of financial management it could have been too daunting. Now the time is just right.

Have you ever wondered why a company with sales in the millions of dollars continually reports staggering net losses, or why a small business faced with overwhelming demand for its services suddenly declares bankruptcy? Many times the reason is not lack of growth, but lack of profitable growth.

> *Gateway Computer, once the third largest distributor of personal computers in the United States, provides a good example of the tribulations companies can confront while working to cultivate profitable growth.*
>
> *Gateway, originally the TIPC Network, was founded by Ted Waitt on a South Dakota farm in 1985. Legend has it Mr. Waitt borrowed $10,000 to start the business and secured the loan with his grandmother's certificate of deposit.*
>
> *Initially the company sold personal computer parts directly to consumers via telephone. Within two years, the company was offering complete computer systems. Gateway's strategy was simple: offer knowledgeable buyers full-featured computer systems for approximately the same price as competitor's stripped down systems by eliminating resellers.*
>
> *Gateway's approach was a success. Annual sales reached over $1 billion by 1992 and $5 billion by 1996. Profitability began*

suffering in 1997, however, as the computer industry suffered from decreasing prices and over supply. The company's sales increased 25% to 6.3 billion in 1997, but profitability decreased by 50% that year.

In 1998 Mr. Waitt decided to make significant changes at Gateway. The firm's headquarters was moved to San Diego, primarily to make it easier to attract qualified personnel. Gateway entered into several strategic alliances with companies such as Sun Microsystems, Office Max and AOL to augment its capacity for new product development and product sales. The company expanded its lines of business to include consulting services. Finally, Gateway opened hundreds of Gateway Country Stores to sell computers at the retail level. The company planned to achieve sales revenues of $25 billion by 2001.

These expansion strategies were considered risky and met with mixed success. The move out of Sioux City changed consumers' perception of Gateway and caused it to lose much of its down home image. Furthermore, experts estimated it cost $1.5 million to launch a Gateway Country store. Financing hundreds of stores put enormous financial stress on the company.

The retail expansion was not successful. In 2004, after several restructurings, Gateway closed all of its Country Stores. Gartner analyst Charles Smulders described the store closings:

It's a positive move for Gateway ... The stores were expensive to run, and margins are very thin in the consumer PC business ... Gateway held a 3.5 percent market share ... Gateway has been losing share for some time ... Gateway was unable to drive enough store traffic to justify the cost of operating the stores ... The margins they were able to make and the volumes they were able to drive just did not match the store investment.

In 2003 Gateway experienced a net loss of $114 million, or 35 cents per share, on revenues of $3.4 billion.

In 2004 Gateway acquired low-cost personal computer maker eMachines, which had annual sales of $1.1 billion and several years of profitable growth. The company was well-known for its product distribution through outlets such as Best Buy and Walmart.

Gateway's retail sales did increase as a result of this merger, and the company achieved market share of over 6% by 2006. While the company is profitable, margins keep getting squeezed. Gateway continues to look for ways to reduce operating costs and increase profitability.[1]

Gateway's struggles are indicative of the balancing act that surrounds growth management. At one time or another virtually every company will experience the pleasures and wrath of intense sales growth. A knowledge and understanding of the fundamentals of healthy growth will help smooth the tumultuous ride.

SALES VOLUME

How could a business otherwise survive without a steady flow of new sales and repeat business? Undoubtedly, growth is the primary driver for healthy business development. Intuitively, we know a certain level of annual growth in sales is needed simply to keep the doors open. However, to build real financial muscle every business has to achieve critical mass in sales revenue.

At critical mass, most businesses will be in a position to exercise significant buying and purchasing leverage. Their size will translate into economic clout and open doors to greater cost savings and price discounts. However, critical mass is a relative concept. A smaller company may have a lower threshold than its larger counterparts.

In the sense, critical mass may require more sales volume than breakeven. For breakeven your profit margin must equal your operating, general and administrative expenses. After the threshold has been achieved, profit margins on any additional sales flow directly to the positive bottom line.

On the other hand, think of critical mass as the magic point on the scale where a company can exercise influence and bargain more favorably with suppliers. More purchasing power alone may offer an economic advantage over less endowed peers. Similarly, price and purchasing advantages are usually extended to businesses with high growth potential. Suppliers offer price discounts to customers who purchase frequently and in increasing volumes, rather than companies that purchase sporadically or in small quantities.

Economic clout goes beyond discounts on merchandise purchases. For example, banks often offer special cost saving in the form of lower fees for loan origination, loan interest, checking and other bank services to commercial clients who utilize a package of banking services. Like many other suppliers of goods and services, financial institutions reward their more lucrative customer relationships.

In terms of resale value, the market price of a high sales volume company will usually be markedly higher than for a similar smaller company. This is especially true in industries that customarily base business values on multiples of annual gross sales revenues. In many cases, a strong volume has the effect of nullifying any significance that might otherwise be attached to a string of financial losses. Ideally, every business should aim for the total package: a handsome top line and profitable bottom line.

Growth Strategies

Devising an effective growth strategy does not mean planning to bring in any and all forms of new business. On the contrary, viable growth strategies focus on attracting and retaining "profitable customers." Generally speaking, quality of new business is just as important as quantity. A basic set of questions that may help to trigger a balanced focus on both quality and quantity are as follows:

How big are your ideal clients?

For commercial clients, consider characteristics such as annual revenues and number of employees. For retail clients, consider household income and household size.

Under what circumstances do clients need to purchase from you?

Selling to a company or individual who needs your product or service is far easier than selling to a potential client who does not see immediate value in your goods.

How often do they purchase and in what quantities?

All businesses love repeat buyers. Knowing who purchases most from you will help you plan your sales and marketing activities and determine when price discounts are advantageous.

Which potential clients can best afford your product or service?

You don't want to waste valuable sales and marketing resources pursuing companies only to find they cannot afford your goods. Similarly, few entrepreneurial businesses have the time or energy to chase slow paying clients.

As the list suggests, the clientele you target naturally dictates many other decisions ranging from promotional media and collateral material to business location and pricing. The more focused your target market is, the more effective your growth strategies are likely to be.

While a full discussion of particular marketing techniques would go far beyond the confines of this book, the more effective approaches usually reflect a combination of direct advertising, word of mouth, customer referrals, price discounts, better service, and consistent quality. Effective selling and marketing are no doubt key to growing sales.

Another a growth strategy that has proven highly effective for many small and large companies is growth by acquisition. Acquisitions of other companies with an attractive customer base, distribution outlets or stellar reputation may be a viable growth technique. The approach can be applied in many different industries.

However, please be forewarned, acquiring another company requires careful investment analysis. Acquisition candidates must be evaluated in depth operationally, financially and legally. In other words, investing in another company to promote growth can also be a high risk proposition. First, the numbers have to make sense. When the acquirer lacks the necessary expertise to conduct a thorough analysis they usually engage a team of specialists for representation.

If any assessment proves positive, a combination of two separate businesses may enable the combined entity to eliminate duplicate expenses and absorb excess capacity. Likewise, the firms may realize economies of scale from blending technical expertise. For these reasons growth through acquisition should never be ruled out even by an entrepreneurial business. Hardly a day goes by when mergers and acquisitions are not reported in local and national business news.

While the average entrepreneurial business may not possess the investment capital of industry giants, growth by acquisition could be a plausible option with the right financing. Investment bankers aggressively pursue opportunities to package acquisition deals that offer major promise. The key question for them is whether the business combination will significantly enhance the earnings power of the companies involved and thereby, attract investor interest.

> *A plausible way to plan business development is by the acquisition of another company that has just the right stuff.*

HEALTHY BUSINESS EXPANSION

Too much or too little growth will wreak havoc on the bottom line of any business. The secret to benefiting from growth lies in distinguishing a healthy versus unhealthy growth. In other words you must have a strong sense of manageable limits. Moreover, when you exceed your company's financing or operating capacity losses and instability and financial loss may ensue.

A massive leap in sales growth can drain cash and drive up short term debt. This could endanger a company's ability to pay ordinary expenses on a timely basis. Similarly, a sudden jump in operating expenses could make it impossible for a growing company to service its debt.

The first test of feasibility is sufficiency of financing resources. Growing without adequate financing is likely to result in financial impairment. Without sufficient internal resources or "bridge financing," working capital will evaporate.

In addition, most companies face a functional restraint dictated by operating capacity. The simplest way to understand this limitation is to think in terms of maximum production capacity measured by the maximum capacity of equipment, physical plant and labor. Like a breakeven exercise you should ask the question for your business: "What levels of production can we comfortably handle?"

In a service enterprise output capacity may not be easy to pinpoint. Metrics may have to be designed based on time studies or average completion of routine customer transactions. In essence, it is important to determine your staff's daily, weekly or monthly limit recognizing over capacity may compromise customer service and quality.

Because conditions are subject to change, manageable growth limits, financing and operating capacities should be monitored and re-evaluated periodically. Remember, exceeding reasonable bounds will tend to jeopardize the overall financial well being of your company.

Boeing Co. learned first hand that spiraling growth can have a crippling effect. Now, they conscientiously tempter growth and resist the temptation to overreach.

The Wall Street Journal reported on Boeings previous challenges:

In 1997, Boeing tried to ramp up production so quickly that suppliers were unable to make parts fast enough. Unfinished planes stacked up at its factories here, forcing managers to shut down production for a month to allow the strained supply chain to catch up. The colossal stumble led to a rare year-end loss and $2.6 billion in charges against earnings over two years.

Building an aircraft requires a reported 367,000 parts from nearly 1,000 suppliers and can take years to complete. Boeing incurs much of the production cost before the customer pays off *the $65 million price, and the delay in delivery of a plane or cancellation of an order by an airline can have devastating effects. Much can change during the time it takes to build a plane, and airlines have been known to cancel orders during recessions such as occurred after September 11, 2001.*

Boeing management does not intend to make the same mistake twice. Although demand for new aircraft is increasing dramatically, the company intends to increase production gradually. According to Scott Carson, head of Boeing's Commercial Airplanes Unit, "Boeing will agree to a jump in production rates only if it can sustain the pace for at least a couple of years.... We don't sell airplanes on the assumption that the factories have infinite ability to produce them."

Now Boeing uses a committee of senior managers from both the production and finance areas of the firm to approve major airline orders and associated delivery timetables. Available capacity at both Boeing and its suppliers is factored into the approval process.

Similarly, Boeing uses a team to manage airport delivery dates and backorders. The company delivered 398 airplanes in 2006, up 41% from 2003 deliveries. Management expects deliveries to increase to 445 and 520 in 2007 and 2008, respectively.

Boeing's cautionary approach is paying off financially. The Commercial Airplanes Unit's operating profit margins reached almost 10% in 2006, up from the 6% achieved in the past. Their self restraint probably best exemplifies the wisdom of controlling growth.[2]

Boeing's lessons are indicative of the perils that uncontrolled growth creates. As a general rule a business should avoid unlimited growth and not set limits of growth strictly in response to demand. Service enterprises also can fall into the trap of becoming demand driven. In the final analysis, growth should never be allowed to outstrip the financing or operating capacity of a business.

INFRASTRUCTURE DEVELOPMENT

Preparing to grow profitably usually entails upgrading systems that support business services and operating production. A strong infrastructure is essential in order to withstand increased demand flow from added business activity. Otherwise, operating bottlenecks and disruptions are bound to occur.

> *Growth should never be allowed to outstrip financing or operating capacity.*

These and other basic support systems facilitate adequate staffing, training, supplies and materials. Critical infrastructure also consist of budget controls, performance benchmarks and system of accounting. Without these prerequisites for managing growth, profitability is virtually impossible.

A strong reporting system is also key to growth management systems serve to prevent a false positive, that is, an erroneous conclusion that efficiency and productivity are at peak levels. Operating only based on what you intuitively think is a profitable platform is a recipe for disaster.

Throughout this book we have largely focused on key parts of business and financial infrastructure. Our study has extended from planning, tracking and monitoring performance to legal structure and risk controls. You do not want to experience a growth spurt without having your house in order.

In order to maintain profits as a business grows accountability is crucial. Albeit the cost and use of resources by specific divisions,

> *Support systems continually test, challenge and monitor productivity, efficiency and performance.*

departments and projects illustrates the need for reliable information and feedback in real time and may make or break the bottom line. Entrepreneurs and CEOs cannot have an oversupply of convenient

Systems should monitor efficiency and profitability by tracking inputs and outputs between divisions, departments and projects.

mechanisms for evaluating their business company-wide on a day-to-day and month-to-month basis.

Highly successful multinational companies like Toyota Motor Corporation are keenly aware of the hazards of rising inefficiency in the face of growth. As noted in a published article Toyota Motor Corporation relies on a close watch over performance, productivity and efficiency to remain on top:

> *Senior managers fear the company will suffer from the same arrogance which has derailed several other international car manufacturers. According to Ken Tomikawa, Toyota Canada president, "The enemy of Toyota is Toyota." Jeremy Cato of Merrill Lynch described Tomikawa's concern as follows:*
>
> *... he worries about the new, young, swaggering Toyota employees who have never experienced bad times and who seem to be comfortable with the idea that Toyota is just naturally superior to all the other auto makers.*
>
> *To avoid complacency, Toyota recently implemented significant improvements in its manufacturing processes and found ways to save substantial development and production costs.[3]*

Toyota's philosophy speaks to the need of the value to continually revisit performance standards and incentives. If not inefficiencies and complacency can undercut profits even in the face of strong sales growth.

PRECAUTIONARY MEASURES

As the information in this chapter suggests growth does not automatically translate to greater financial return. Many companies experience strong consistent sales growth but show steadily declining profits. If a CEO does not spot trouble signs early, growth will only worsen earnings.

On the other hand, with sound planning and oversight, growth is the best avenue for maximizing financial returns. However, certain precautions must be taken. First, pricing and cost controls have to implemented. Additionally, cash from operations must be closely monitored and supplemented from time to time to maintain positive cash flow.

During a peak growth cycle you must be on guard for financial deterioration in the form of late payments to key vendors, and build up accounts receivable. As growth peaks, maintaining stability will be a day-to-day challenge.

Financial percentages and ratios should be monitored frequently. Indicators that gauge working capital, accounts receivable turnover and cash flow coverage should be tracked closely and routinely.

Managing growth also requires making enhancements and upgrades to your business structure along the way and preferably in advance. Many companies with high growth potential falter because these needs go unaddressed until the eleventh hour.

Preparing an updated business plan is also highly recommended. A variety of management needs and requirements will likely change in a significant way. Your organizational blueprint should be complete with an organizational chart depicting any necessary changes in the division of duties and responsibilities. Organizational preparation also entails modifying written policies and procedures to better foster a productive work place.

Likewise, technology upgrades are essential. "IT strategy" is highly recommended. Similarly, the personnel recruitment, training and development plan adjustments will be necessitated. Growth normally demands a more diverse set of job skills and staff composition.

Last but not least, growth management entails implementing financial safeguards known as internal controls. These controls represent a specific subset of financial controls aimed primarily at protecting assets from mishandling, theft or fraud and at assuring accuracy in financial accounting and reporting. Internal controls represent a highly functional system of checks and balances that focus on detecting financial errors and irregularities.

THE HOMESTRETCH

For better or for worse, for richer or for poorer, entrepreneurs and CEOs have to take charge of the financial well-being of their company. Many business veterans wish they had become intricately involved in the financial affairs from the get go.

As in any athletic endeavor, ultimately the head coach is responsible for getting the team ready to compete at a high level. They may delegate certain duties to assistants and team captains but at the end of the day the head coach will be held accountable. It is a fine line between maximizing player talent and controlling team performance.

In an interview for Babson Insight, Herb Kelleher, CEO of Southwest Airlines discussed the methods it uses to promote the best performance.

"...We use scenario planning. We might ask 'what happens if a certain airline significantly contracts its fleet?' In response we pull together our ideas on how we might respond. You just can't predict what may happen and that's why I say: ready, aim, fire because opportunity won't be there unless you act quickly. It doesn't have to be perfect when you start it. This is what prevents many people from being quick, they want to be perfect. We'd rather go ahead imperfectly and improve as we go."[4]

The Road to MegaSuccess was aimed to help you redesign and improve your financial management game plan. Armed with knowledge, skill and proven strategies for success, I am confident you will indeed grow profitably. For ease of planning your moves in the future, the next and final chapter provides a graphic recap of the critical elements for enriching the bottom line.

> *The Road to Mega Success is a never ending journey.*

NOTABLE REFLECTIONS AT A GLANCE

✦ Profitable growth requires meticulous planning and oversight with the following guiding principles:

✦ Controlling growth means balancing financing and operating capacity.

✦ Profitable growth produces positive top and bottom lines.

✦ Sound management minimizes internal and external resources.

✦ Performance assessment must be a top priority.

✦ Successful businesses invest in growth and business development.

CHAPTER THIRTEEN

Develop Muscle Memory...
Practice the Mantra

| *The Journey* |

Just days before opening the door of the new business BJ received a call from by a national business broker. The broker had information that Matrix's most formidable regional competitor would be up for sale in less than a month. He encouraged BJ to seriously consider making a purchase offer.

On the other hand, already deeply immersed in the new deal with Taylor BJ was conflicted about taking any additional investment risks. Nevertheless, he felt compelled at least to carefully evaluate the feasibility of the business acquisition. He thought of the basic process of analysis used in planning the joint venture with Taylor, or the mantra for success.

By combining Matrix's sales volume, distribution network, and market share would double. The financial rewards could include much greater economies to scale in purchasing inventory, more efficient operating equipment, more convenient warehousing and other operational advantages.

On the other hand, BJ knew the deal would require considerable financing.

As he thought more about the possible acquisition BJ realized the mantra would work from one deal to another. Essentially, you have to repeat the mantra to ensure success.

I. SET THE RIGHT COURSE

- Set the Course for Profitable Growth

- Establish a Winning Financial Game Plan

- Exercise Close Oversight

- Aim for a Healthy Bottom Line

- Effective Management and Coaching are Key to MegaSuccess

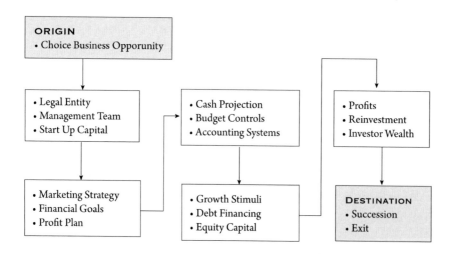

II. Avoid the Classic Pitfalls

- The Mirage—Avoid the illusion of profitability

- Structural Losses—Deficit pricing and flawed cost estimation amounts to built-in losses

- Crippling Growth—growth on the back of no or slow paying accounts robs cash flow

- Crisis Culture—The emergency response mode of management is less effective than a proactive approach

- Erratic Oversight—Monitoring financial performance should be an obsession, not a sporadic exercise.

- Restricted Comfort Zone—Over dependence on a single product, service or customer leaves a business vulnerable financially

- Lack of Profit Planning—Utilize a methodical rather than simply an intuitive approach to grow a positive bottom line

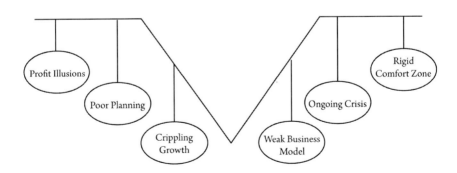

III. PLOT A POSITIVE CASH FLOW

- Short-term business survival depends on a positive cash flow

- Billing, collection, purchases, payroll and operating disbursements shall all be in sync by design

- A cash flow projection is the best tool for plotting your game plan

- Improving cash flow requires minimizing collection float and maximizing disbursement float

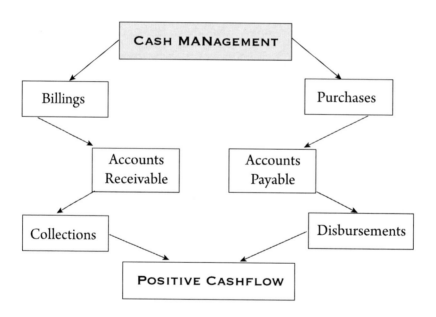

IV. "Net" Trumps Gross

- Focus on growing the bottom line not just sales volume

- Breakeven is a key determinant of minimum sales volume needed to cover expenses

- Profit modeling delineates direct and indirect costs to enhance profit planning

- Profit margins on products or services in excess of breakeven flow to the bottom line

- B/E sales can be adjusted by variations in price and/or cost

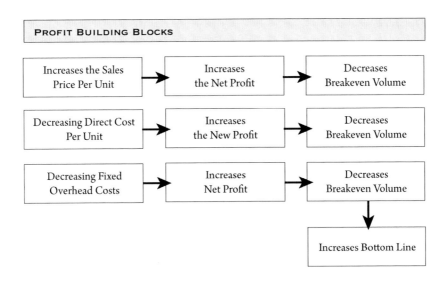

PROFIT BUILDING BLOCKS

Increases the Sales Price Per Unit	Increases the Net Profit	Decreases Breakeven Volume
Decreasing Direct Cost Per Unit	Increases the New Profit	Decreases Breakeven Volume
Decreasing Fixed Overhead Costs	Increases Net Profit	Decreases Breakeven Volume
		Increases Bottom Line

V. Examine Your Financials

- A comprehensive financial statement will best tell your story

- Generally Accepted Accounting Principles (GAAP) are the set of universal standards for financial reporting

- Financial vitality is widely recognized by profit & loss, assets and liabilities, and cash flow

- Prospective lenders and investors utilize financial statements as a litmus test in making financing decisions

Managerial Uses

Income Statement	Cash Flow Statement	Balance Sheet
Net Earnings Profit Potential Financial Performance	Sources and Uses of Cash	Assets Liabilities Equity

VS

Financier's Uses

Income Statement	Cash Flow Statement	Balance Sheet
Net Earnings Profit Potential Financial Results	Sources and Uses of Cash	Asset Mix Debt Load Owner's Equity

VI. Build Economic Stamina

- Financial well-being is generally measured by certain key vital signs

- Standard financial indicators are reflective of good health and fitness

- Efficiency, liquidity and financial return are among the primary types of performance measures

- Ratios and percentages allow for comparison with industry norms and trends

- Internal controls promote both compliance and efficiency through a defined set of checks and balances

- Audits, reviews and compilations serve to boost the credibility of your financial statements

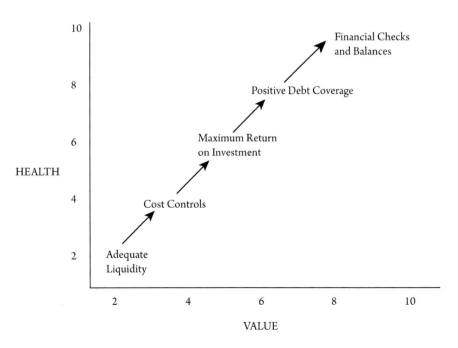

VII. FINANCE YOUR DREAM

- Access to capital is critical for financing growth and expansion

- Sources of capital come in two varieties, debt and equity

- Capital needs are usually driven by business development, build up in accounts receivables, purchase of business equipment, land acquisition and business combinations

- Your financing strategy should reflect both current and future needs based on your business plan

- Financing structure should align repayment obligations with expected future income streams

- An up to date financing dossier is critical for facilitating a quick turnaround

FINANCING ALTERNATIVES	
Debt	**Equity**
Lines of Credit	Owner's Capital
Term Loan	Angel Investors
Asset-Based Receivables Financing	Venture Capital Investors
Mortgage Borrowing	Public Offerings

VIII. Instill Peak Performance

- To sustain a high level of profitability a company must be performance driven

- Concrete financial benchmarks set the stage for peak performance

- Performance measures and standards usually come in the form of stated criteria such as sales, production, profit, etc.

- Activity budgets track the level of operating activity needed to generate a positive bottom line

- Financial budgeting evaluates performance based on monetary outcomes

- Variance analysis vis a vis an activity or financial budget model helps identify trouble spots

- Micro-managing high impact drivers is a key part of manufacturing peak performance

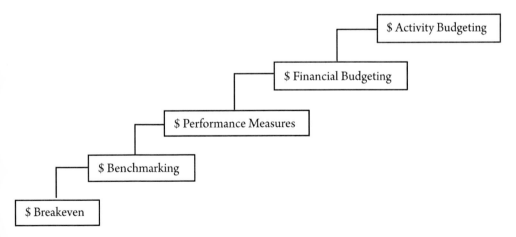

IX. Tighten Up Legally

- A solid legal infrastructure is the foundation for asset protection

- Limited legal liability protection mitigates risk of personal loss to investors

- A legal business entity is a viable form of self-defense in case of business related lawsuits

- Every teaming relationship should be embraced by a formal legal document

- A buy-sell agreement serves to specify a method of valuation in the event of a transition of ownership as well as other agreed upon terms of management operation

- Corporate bylaws and LLC operating agreements provide another way to tighten the organizational business structure

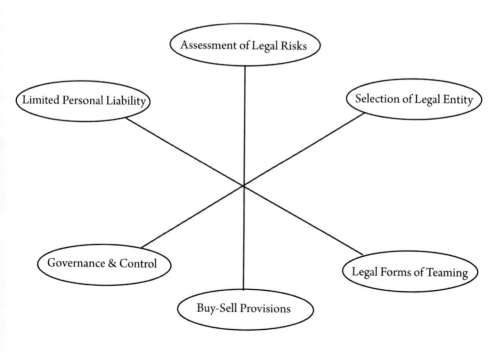

X. DOWNSIZE BUSINESS RISKS

- If you do not control risks, they will control you

- It pays to actively manage business risks

- Cash reserves enhance an entrepreneurs ability to withstand periods of high volatility

- Insurance coverage serves to soften the financial impact of loss due to death, disability or serious illness

- Boards of advisors and directors help prevent mental fatigue and stagnation

- Succession plans involve exit strategies via business sale, transfer or other type of business disposition

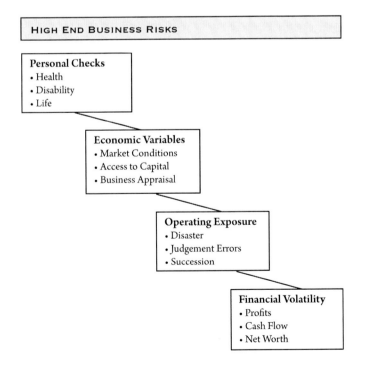

HIGH END BUSINESS RISKS

Personal Checks
- Health
- Disability
- Life

Economic Variables
- Market Conditions
- Access to Capital
- Business Appraisal

Operating Exposure
- Disaster
- Judgement Errors
- Succession

Financial Volatility
- Profits
- Cash Flow
- Net Worth

XI. EARMARK STRATEGIC PRIORITIES

- The most successful businesses earmark their strategic priorities

- Long-term survival may depend on adequate liquidity in the future

- Earnings and profits are not fully available for distribution to investors

- Set asides for seed money and dollars for business reinvestment are essential to remain competitive

- A quarterly income tax deposit minimizes exposure at year-end

- A reserve for debt retirement helps offset long term obligations

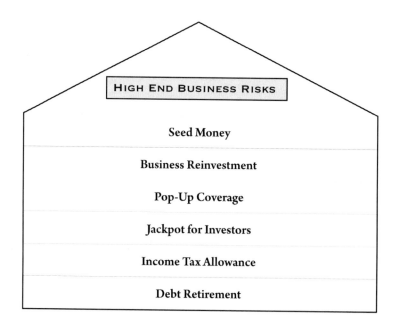

HIGH END BUSINESS RISKS

Seed Money

Business Reinvestment

Pop-Up Coverage

Jackpot for Investors

Income Tax Allowance

Debt Retirement

XII. Champion Profitable Growth

- Profitable growth balances sales, growth, cash flow and profit

- A strong financial support system is key to championing profitable growth

- Unmanaged growth undermines financial stability

- Strategic planning serves to sustain profitable performance over the long-term

- Proof in the pudding is finishing in the black financially

The Road to MegaSuccess

+ Sales Strategies

+ Profit Parameters

+ Cash Flow Support

+ Financing Capacity

+ Internal Control Systems

+ Performance Oversight

+ Risk Management
_____

= Profitable Growth

ENRICHING THE BOTTOM LINE

THE MANTRA

1. Set the Right Course

2. Avoid the Classic Pitfalls

3. Plot a Positive Cash Flow

4. "Net" Trumps Gross

5. Examine Your Financials

6. Build Economic Stamina

7. Finance the Dream

8. Instill Peak Performance

9. Tighten Up Legally

10. Downsize Business Risks

11. Earmark Strategic Priorities

12. Champion Profitable Growth

GLOSSARY

Assets—Includes both tangible and intangible items of value held by the company for future benefit. Generally, most assets held are exchangeable or saleable for some amount of money. For accounting purposes asset values are generally reported at the lower of purchase price or market value.

Audit—Generally, describes the process wherein a CPA examines, on a test basis, evidence supporting the balances, values and disclosures reported in the financial statements. An audit includes assessing the accounting principles used for significant estimates made by management, as well as evaluation of the overall financial statement presentation. Audits provide a reasonable basis for a CPA's opinion on whether the financial statements are presented fairly in all material respects.

Balance Sheet—Addresses liquidity and changes in net worth via reports that detail company assets, liabilities and equity. A balance sheet will pinpoint financial status at the end of a month, quarter or year.

Budget—A budget is a compilation of financial estimates focusing on expected future sources and uses of funds. A budget should be used as a management tool for overseeing costs of operation and for establishing a plan to maximize available resources. Most organizations and businesses prepare separate budgets for operations versus expenditures for equipment, improvements and other capital expenditures.

Capital—Refers to funds invested by owners and shareholders to support building and growing a business enterprise. Adequate capital serves to relieve pressure to ramp up sales faster than is reasonable or desirable.

Cash Flow Statement—Breakdown of cash activity by listing all sources and uses of cash tied to operations, capital infusions or loans. This report captures cash activity that occurs during a month, quarter or year.

Compilation—Represents financial information reported on by a CPA. The pertinent data comes in the form of financial statement that is the representation of management (the owners). For purposes of a compilation, CPA's do not audit or review the financial statements and, accordingly, do not express an opinion or any other form of assurance on them.

Equity—Represents net dollar difference between the stated values of the company's assets and liabilities.

Expenses—The costs fully incurred by the business and typically are divided into costs of goods sold (items needed to produce a product or service) and operating expenses (items such as rent, salaries, insurance and advertising incurred in managing the business).

Financial Statements—Generally, this term refers to a balance sheet, income statement and statement of cash flows. The reports are universally recognized as the most comprehensive way to report financial condition, results of operation and cash flow especially when prepared according to Generally Accepted Accounting Principles (GAAP).

Income Statement—Measures profitability—revenues from sales less costs of products or services and any other expenses necessary to operate the business. Normally covers a month, quarter, or year.

Profit Margin—The difference between the unit selling price of a product or service and direct costs to make the product or render the services.

Revenues—Comprise gross funds received in dollars or amounts billed by a company to its customers for sale of goods and services.

Review—An inspection conducted by a CPA comprised of inquiries of company personnel and analytical procedures applied to financial data. It is substantially less in scope than an audit in accordance with generally accepted auditing standards, the objective of which is the expression of an opinion regarding the financial statements taken as a whole.

Sources of Cash—Include net income, proceeds from bank loans, and contributions by owners as well as sale of assets.

Uses of Cash—Include payment of operating expenses, loan payments, equipment purchases, and real estate purchases investments in other assets. Liabilities Legally enforceable claims and financial obligations for vendor invoices, taxes and outstanding loans.

ENDNOTES

Chapter Two: Evade the Fault Line ... Prevent the Classic Pitfalls

1. United States, Small Business Administration, "Advocacy: The Voice of Small Business in Government 2006 Frequently Asked Questions," June 2006, July 15, 2006 http://www.sba.gov/advo/stats/sbfaq.pdf.

The U.S. Small Business Administration reported the following with regard to business formations and closures:

Just fewer than 600,000 new businesses with employees are formed each year, and approximately 550,000 firms with employees close each year.

Approximately two-thirds of new employers survive at least two years; however, only one-half make it four years or more.

2. "Eisner Abruptly Shuts Down," Baltimore Sun, November 11, 2006

Chapter Three: Adopt the Golden Rule ... "Net" Trumps Gross

1. How to Make Money the Buffet Way," U.S. News and World Report, August 6, 2007, page 49.

Chapter Four: Adopt the Golden Rule... Net Trumps Gross

1. Seeking Perfect Prices, CEO Tears Up the Rules," *Wall Street Journal*, March 27, 2007.

Chapter Seven: Accelerate the Breakthrough... Finance Your Dream

1. Google Corporate Milestones, January 2006, http://www.google.com/intl/en/corporate/history.html, March 15, 2006.

2. MMG Financial Funds, Meridian Management Group, Inc., http://www.mmggroup.com/funds_mmgv_01.html, http://www.mmggroup.com/funds_mmgv_02.html, and http://www.mmggroup.com/funds_mmgv_03.html, March 15, 2006

Chapter Eight: Inspect What You Expect... Instill Peak Performance

1. Scott Martin, "How Apple Beat Tiffany," *Red Herring*, http://www.red-herring.com/Article.aspx?a=200332&hed=How+Appl..., July 24, 2007.

2. Jena McGregor, "Leading Listener: Trader Joe's," *Fast Company.com*, http://www.fastcompany.com/magazine/87/customer-traderjoes.htm, October 2004.

3. Eric Monnoyer and Stefan Spang, "Manufacturing Lessons for Service Industries: An Interview with Axe's Claude Brunet," *McKinsey Quarterly* (Spring 2005), 11.

4. Monnoyer and Spang, "Manufacturing Lessons for Service Industries," 12.

5. *Supply Chain Security Best Practices Catalog, Customs-Trade Partnership Against Terrorism*, U.S. Customs and Borer Protection, January 2006, iii.

Chapter Eleven: Gradually Stockpile Reserves... Earmark Strategic Priorities

1. "Behind Microsoft's Bid to Gain Cutting Edge," *Wall Street Journal*, July 30, 2007.

2. "Looking Forward: S&T for the 21st Century," National Research Council Canada, http://www.nrc-cnrc.gc.ca/aboutUs/ren/nrc-foreshight_10_e.html, September 16, 2005.

3. "Economy Slows But May Hold Seeds of Growth," *Wall Street Journal*, April 28, 2007.

4. World Population Prospects: The 2006 Revision," *Fact Sheet, Series A*, United Nations Department of Economic and Social Affairs, Population Division, Population Estimates and Projections Section, March 2007.

Chapter Twelve: Champion Profitable Growth... Finish in the Black

1. Jason Dedrick, Kenneth L. Kraemer and Bryan MacQuarrie, "Gateway Computer: Using E-Commerce to Move 'Beyond the Box' and to Move More Boxes," Center for Research on information Technology and Organizations, University of California, Irvine, February 2001, and Susan Kichinskas, "Gateway Stores Put Out to Pasture," *Internetnews.com*, http://www.internetnews.com/bus-news/print.php/3334901, April 2, 2004.

2. "Burned by Last Boom, Boeing Curbs Its Pace," *Wall Street Journal*, March 26, 2007.

3. Jeremy Cato, "Toyota's Global Strategy Looks Inward," in ToyotaNation.com, http://www.toyotanation.com/forum/showthread.php?1=54954, October 28, 2004.

4. Allan Cohen, James Watkinson and Jenny Boone, "Herb Kelleher Talks about How Southwest Airlines Grew from Entrepreneurial Startup to Industry Leadership," Babson Insight, http://www.babsoninsight.com/contentmgr/showdetails.php/id/829, Babson University.

LOUIS G. HUTT, JR., ESQ., C.P.A.

Louis G. Hutt, Jr. is a native of St. Louis, Missouri. He graduated from Washington University with a Bachelor of Science in Business Administration and joined the audit staff of Ernst and Young Certified Public Accountants. While with Ernst and Young, Hutt was selected to serve as the firm's Visiting Professor of Accounting at Morgan State University.

Upon completing his executive teaching assignment, Hutt attended the University of Maryland School of Law. While there, he interned with the Securities Division of the Maryland Attorney General's Office and clerked for the Honorable Chief Judge Robert Bell who is now Chief Judge of the Maryland Court of Appeals. After completing law school, Hutt established The Law Office of Louis G. Hutt, Jr. and Bennett, Hutt and Co., L.L.C., Certified Public Accountants.

His law practice focuses on representation in tax controversies, contract negotiation, business acquisitions, and business law planning involving the formation of legal entities including tax exempt organizations. Bennett, Hutt and Co., provides executive level management training as well as business, tax and management advisory services to an array of entrepreneurs, professional offices, professional sports, and different regulated organizations. Offices are maintained in Columbia, Maryland and Albuquerque, New Mexico.

Hutt is a weekly guest on XM 169 morning radio talk show (The Madison Show) from Washington D.C. He has been recognized as the Distinguished Alumni of the School of Business by Washington University;

U.S. Small Business Administration as Accounting Advocate of the Year; Waring-Mitchell Law Society's Distinguished Member of the Community Award; Practitioner of the Year by University of Maryland's Black Law Students Association; recipient of NAACP Business Award; and Alpha Kappa Alpha Sorority's Meritorious Service Award.

Louis is also a proud member of Alpha Phi Alpha Fraternity, Inc.

300311-2-250-60W